W9-DFT-555

DISCARD

CHICAGO PUBLIC LIBRARY
BEVERLY BRANCH
1962 W. 95th STREET
CHICAGO, IL 60643

Tarsus
Alexandria
(Alexandretta)
Coris
Ravendal
Manbij
Iron Bridge (Pons Ferri)
Artasium
Aleppo
Rakka
St. Simeon
Antioch
1098-1268
Zerdan
ANTIOCH
Albara
Laodicea
Marra
D O M I N I O N
Gibellum
Apamea
Famagusta
Margat
Chastel Blanc
Hamah
O F   T H E
Tortosa
Mons Ferrandus
Tadmor
Chastel Rouge
Homs (Emesa)
A T A B E K S
Tripoli
1109-1289
Crac des Chevaliers
Arcas
Botroun
Baalbec
A
35 Sidon
1110
Gibilet
Sarepta
Belfort
Beirut
Tyre
1124
Toron
Banu
Sidon
1110
Damascus
Montfort
Tyre
1124
Banias
St. Jean
d'Acre
1104-1187
1191-1291
Safed
Castle
Jacob
an d'Acre
1104-1187
1191-1291
Sea of Galilee
Adratum
Cayphas
Hattin
Sea of
Galilee
Castrum
Peregrinorum
Tiberias
aesarea
1101
Bostra
Nazareth
Gado
Arsuf
Assalt
Belvoir
Jaffa
1099
Caesarea
Baisan
zotus
calon
Jerusalem
1099-1187-1229-1244
Sebaste
Gaza
Arsuf
Neapolis
(Nablus)
Jaffa
1099
Mirabel
Assa
Kerak
Lydda
Jericho
Ramleh
Ibelin
Jerusalem
1099-1187 1229 1244
Montreal
(Mons Regalis)
Blanche
garde
Bethlehem
Segor
Gaza
Hebron
C. - County
P. - Principality.
The dates are those
of conquest or period

CHICAGO, IL 60643

KNIGHTS OF JERUSALEM

THE CRUSADING ORDER
OF HOSPITALLERS 1100–1565

OSPREY
PUBLISHING

CHICAGO PUBLIC LIBRARY
BEVERLY BRANCH
1962 W. 95th STREET
CHICAGO, IL 60643

KNIGHTS OF JERUSALEM

THE CRUSADING ORDER
OF HOSPITALLERS 1100–1565

DAVID NICOLLE

First published in Great Britain in 2008 by Osprey Publishing, Midland House,
West Way, Botley, Oxford, OX2 0PH, United Kingdom.
443 Park Avenue South, New York, NY 10016, USA.
Email: info@ospreypublishing.com

© 2008 David Nicolle

All rights reserved. Apart from any fair dealing for the purpose of private study, research, criticism or review, as permitted under the Copyright, Designs and Patents Act, 1988, no part of this publication may be reproduced, stored in a retrieval system, or transmitted in any form or by any means, electronic, electrical, chemical, mechanical, optical, photocopying, recording or otherwise, without the prior written permission of the copyright owner. Enquiries should be addressed to the Publishers.

Every attempt has been made by the Publishers to secure the appropriate permissions for materials reproduced in this book. If there has been any oversight we will be happy to rectify the situation and a written submission should be made to the Publishers.

A CIP catalogue record for this book is available from the British Library.

ISBN-13: 978 1 84603 080 2

Page layout by Ken Vail Graphic Design, Cambridge, UK
Index by Alison Worthington
Typeset in Truesdell and Centaur MT
Originated by PDQ Media, UK
Printed in China through Worldprint Ltd

08 09 10 11 12   10 9 8 7 6 5 4 3 2 1

For a catalogue of all books published by Osprey please contact:

NORTH AMERICA
Osprey Direct, c/o Random House Distribution Center
400 Hahn Road, Westminster, MD 21157, USA
E-mail: info@ospreydirect.com

ALL OTHER REGIONS
Osprey Direct UK, P.O. Box 140, Wellingborough, Northants, NN8 2FA, UK
E-mail: info@ospreydirect.co.uk

www.ospreypublishing.com

Front cover: Knight Hospitaller by Christa Hook © Osprey Publishing Ltd
Back cover: Louis IX lands at Damietta, in the *Livres des Faits de Monseigneur Saint Louis*, f. 36v, MS. Fr. 2829, Bibliothèque Nationale de France, Paris
Title page: akg images/Visioars

R0429856391

CONTENTS

Chronology

c.1080	Establishment of the Hospital of St John in Jerusalem under Islamic rule.
1095	Pope Urban II preaches the First Crusade.
1099	First Crusade captures Jerusalem; the Blessed Gerard traditionally becomes the first Master of the Order of St John of Jerusalem under Christian rule.
1113	Pope Paschal II recognizes the Hospital of St John in Jerusalem as an Order of the Church; the Blessed Gerard actually becomes first Master of the Order.
1119–20	Order of the Knights Templar founded.
1126	First reference to a constable of the Hospitallers.
1128	Order of the Templars officially recognized by the Church.
c.1130	Composition of the first Rule of the Order of Hospitallers.
c.1135–54	Hospitallers awarded 'exemption', thus becoming free from interference by local religious authorities.
1136	Castle of Bayt Jibrin granted to Hospitallers.
1144	Imad al-Din Zangi retakes Edessa from crusaders; Crac des Chevaliers and four smaller castles given to the Hospitallers.
1145–47	Preaching of Second Crusade in Europe.
1146	Imad al-Din Zangi succeeded by Nur al-Din.
1147–48	Second Crusade defeated in Anatolia and outside Damascus; first unclear reference to a brother-knight of the Hospitallers.
c.1150	Construction of Hospitaller castle at Belmont.
1153	Kingdom of Jerusalem takes Ascalon from Fatimids of Egypt.
1154	Nur al-Din seizes control of Damascus.
1163–69	Five attacks on Egypt by Kingdom of Jerusalem; definite emergence of Hospitaller brethren-in-arms.
1168–72	Construction of Hospitaller castle of Belvoir.
1169	Saladin takes control of Egypt for Nur al-Din of Syria.
1174	Death of Nur al-Din; Saladin takes control of Damascus.
1177	Crusader States defeat Saladin at Mont Gisard; from this date most convents of Hospitaller Sisters are separated from male convents.
1186	Castle of Marqab given to the Hospitallers.
1187	Saladin crushes Kingdom of Jerusalem at battle of Hattin; Saladin retakes Jerusalem.
1188	Rule written for the Hospitaller Sisters in Aragon.
1191–92	King Richard I of England on Third Crusade, gains Cyprus from Byzantine Empire; Third Crusade fails to recapture Jerusalem; Hospitallers move their headquarters to Acre.
1198	Order of the Teutonic Knights officially recognized as a Military Order.
1202	Severe earthquake damages Crac des Chevaliers after which Hospitallers decide on major reconstruction and enlargement; Order of the Sword Brothers established in the Baltic; Fourth Crusade diverted to conquer Byzantine capital of Constantinople.
1211	Teutonic Knights given frontier region in Transylvania by King of Hungary as first Military Order 'state within a state'.

Hospitaller brothers at mass during an earthquake (Obsidionis Rhodie Urbis Descriptio by William Caoursin, f.120v, MS. Lat. 6067, Bibliothèque Nationale de France, Paris)

1217–21	Fifth Crusade defeated in Egypt.
1229	Jerusalem ceded to the Kingdom of Jerusalem by treaty.
1239	Crusade led by the Count of Champagne defeated at the battle of Gaza; Pierre de Vieille Bride becomes Master of the Order.
1244	Jerusalem retaken by Muslims (Khwarazmians); Kingdom of Jerusalem defeated at La Forbie.
1250	Crusade of King (St) Louis of France defeated in Egypt.
1256–58	Civil war in Kingdom of Jerusalem.
1260	Mamluks of Egypt defeat Mongol invaders at 'Ayn Jalut in Palestine.
1263–68	Mamluks devastate Nazareth, retake Caesarea, Arsuf, Saphet, Jaffa, Belfort and Antioch.
1271	Mamluks retake Chastel Blanc, Crac des Chevaliers and Montfort; Prince Edward of England arrives in Palestine on crusade.
1274	Hostile criticism results in a proposal to unify all Military Orders, but this is not adopted.
1277	Crisis in Kingdom of Jerusalem over the recognition of Charles of Anjou as king; civil war in County of Tripoli (1277–83).
1285	Mamluks retake Marqab.
1287–89	Mamluks retake Latakia and Tripoli.
1291	Mamluks retake Acre, Sidon and Beirut; Latin Christians abandon Tortosa and Château Pélerin; end of the Crusader States in the Middle East.

1299	Northern castle of Roche Guillaume falls to the Mamluks.
1302	Mamluks retake Ruad island off Syrian coast; probable end of independent Latin authority in Jbayl.
1306	Hospitallers begin invasion of Byzantine island of Rhodes.
1307	Pope Clement V orders the arrest of all Templars.
1309	Hospitaller headquarters moved to Rhodes.
1311–12	Turkish counter-attacks on Rhodes.
1312	Suppression of the Templars, most of their estates allocated to the Hospitallers; Hospitaller naval victory over the Turks; Hospitallers gain first foothold on the Anatolian mainland.
1318–19	Turkish counter-attacks on Rhodes.
1319	Hospitaller and Genoese fleet destroys a Turkish flotilla off Ephesus; island of Kos lost to the Turks but Lerro gained from Byzantines.
c.1337	Hospitallers regain Kos.
1344	Hospitallers join papal league in the capture of Izmir from Turks.
1347	Hospitaller ships join others in defeating a Turkish flotilla off Imbroz.
1348	Plague hits Rhodes.
1356	Hospitallers try to establish themselves on the Greek mainland.

1359	Hospitaller ships join others in defeating a Turkish flotilla off the Dardanelles.	1404	Hospitallers abandon Corinth.
1361	Hospitallers join King Peter of Cyprus in an attack on Antalya.	c.1407	Hospitallers take and fortify Bodrum.
1365	Hospitallers take part in crusader destruction of Alexandria.	1426	Mamluks invade Cyprus and impose their suzerainty.
1374	Hospitallers made responsible for the defence of crusader-held Izmir.	1428	Hospitallers renew truce with the Mamluks.
1376–81	Disastrous Hospitaller invasion of Italo-Greek Despotate of Epiros.	1440	Mamluks raid Castellorizo and Rhodes.

1359   Hospitaller ships join others in defeating a Turkish flotilla off the Dardanelles.

1361   Hospitallers join King Peter of Cyprus in an attack on Antalya.

1365   Hospitallers take part in crusader destruction of Alexandria.

1374   Hospitallers made responsible for the defence of crusader-held Izmir.

1376–81   Disastrous Hospitaller invasion of Italo-Greek Despotate of Epiros.

1381   Hospitallers abandon their lease on the crusader Principality of Achaea.

1383   'Anti-Master' Riccardo Caracciolo appointed by Pope Urban VI but not acknowledged in Rhodes (resigns in 1395).

1386   Hospitallers buy the Angevin claim to Achaea but are unable to impose their authority.

1396   Hospitallers take part in crusade which is defeated at Nicopolis by the Ottomans.

1397   Hospitallers occupy Corinth and help defend the Peloponnese against the Ottomans.

1401   Crusader Prince of Achaea attacks Hospitaller possessions on the Greek mainland.

1402   Timur-i Lenk captures Izmir.

1403   Hospitaller treaty with the Mamluk Sultanate allows the Order to rebuild its infirmary in Jerusalem; Crusader Duke of Athens attacks Hospitaller possessions on the Greek mainland.

1404   Hospitallers abandon Corinth.

c.1407   Hospitallers take and fortify Bodrum.

1426   Mamluks invade Cyprus and impose their suzerainty.

1428   Hospitallers renew truce with the Mamluks.

1440   Mamluks raid Castellorizo and Rhodes.

1443   Mamluks capture Castellorizo and hold it for some months.

1444   Mamluk invasion of Rhodes withdraws after a 40-day siege of the city; Hospitaller peace treaty with the Mamluks renewed.

1451   Hospitaller ships attack Karaman in alliance with the Mamluks and Lutfi Bey of Alanya.

1455   Ottomans raid Rhodes.

1479   Failure of negotiations between Hospitallers and Ottoman Sultanate.

1522   Ottomans conquer Rhodes.

1523   Hospitaller headquarters moved to Italy.

1528   Hospitallers help defend Spanish-held Tripoli.

1530   Hospitaller headquarters moved to Malta.

1531   Hospitaller expedition takes Modon in Greece but immediately loses it to the Ottomans again.

1541   Hospitallers take part in unsuccessful Spanish attack on Algiers.

1551   Hospitallers lose Tripoli.

1565   Unsuccessful Ottoman invasion of Malta.

Introduction

FEUDAL SOCIETY, CHRISTIANITY AND VIOLENCE

The medieval Military Orders, including the Hospitallers, represented a distinctive and in many ways separate aspect of medieval life, but they were also a reflection of the society in which they lived. This society has often been described, simplistically, as being feudal. It was based upon a theoretical pyramid of responsibilities with a ruler at the top, various layers of aristocracy in between, and 'unfree' but not enslaved serf-peasants at the bottom. In reality, this theoretical structure never existed in such an idealized form, not even in 12th- or 13th-century France, which is often seen as being as feudal a society as one could find. Still, the model is a useful one for understanding something of the contemporary society and its structures.

The organization of the Church had a comparable hierarchy of responsibilities and existed alongside the secular hierarchy with which it was frequently in competition. The military orders epitomized this competition. They were monastic, but drew their members from an aristocratic, warrior elite.

THE RISE OF THE MILITARY ORDERS AND 'HOLY WAR'

From the 10th to mid-12th centuries the warrior classes of Western Europe had been under especially strong Church influence and it was during this period that the concept of the 'Christian warrior' and his 'struggle against the infidels' emerged. The papacy had always employed its own local military forces, but during the 11th century the popes began recruiting substantial armies not only to defend themselves but also to combat their rivals, most notably the emerging Norman kingdom in southern Italy. These troops were, however, little different from those employed by any other ruler.

The Military Orders that were founded and flourished during the 12th century were very different. They consisted of militarized 'warrior monks' and

OPPOSITE
'The Knights of Christ' on a painted panel that forms part of the Altarpiece of the Holy Lamb by Jan van Eyck. In addition to being a superb illustration of mid-15th-century German-style armour, this painting seems to represent the great Military Orders, with that of the Hospitallers of St John being on the left. (in situ, church of St Bavo, Ghent, Belgium/The Bridgeman Art Library)

there were always some members of the clergy who doubted the propriety of warriors being so closely identified with the Church. Even these critics, however, normally accepted the use of violence against infidels, pagans or schismatics and recognized that participation in a crusade was a valid method of remitting the participants' sins. Others feared that the Military Orders, because of their methods of recruitment as much as their warlike activities, posed a threat to the exclusive character of traditional monasticism. In contrast, the papacy almost immediately recognized the usefulness of the Military Orders and justified their violence as being 'preventative'. The popes were also aware that such Orders gave potential troublemakers within the knightly class something useful to do. They were initially less willing to see the originally charitable medical Order of the Hospitallers being militarized than to accept the warlike role of the Templars, who had been founded for just that purpose; but secular rulers had no such doubts and were, for several centuries, enthusiastic supporters and promoters of Hospitallers, Templars and other Military Orders that were established in subsequent decades. Nevertheless everyone, including the Military Orders themselves, accepted that membership of such orders offered less spiritual merit than membership of traditional contemplative orders, old or new.

The religious and spiritual justification for the Military Orders was essentially the same as that of the crusades themselves. It was largely based upon what is often called St Augustine's radical pessimism, which claimed that perfect peace was impossible on earth, but that violence was only sanctioned to maintain justice or impose peace. Furthermore, any sin inherent in the waging of unjust war fell upon the ruler, not upon his men. War was seen not as a consequence of sin but as a remedy for it. Thus the punishment of wrongdoers was an act of love. It was in this intellectual atmosphere that the higher clergy of the Church had themselves become increasingly militarized by the 10th century and this in its turn led to the crusading movement. The focus of the crusade against Islam was also justified on the grounds that the Church had declared Muslims to be *summa culpabilis*, 'the most blameworthy' of peoples.

Another feature of these centuries was an increasing concern with the concepts of Just and Unjust War. In simple terms, to take part in Just War was 'allowed by God' whereas to take part in Holy War was 'commanded by God'. The crusades, though, seem to have been rooted in a third idea of war, the legal concept of *Bellum Romanum* (Roman War), which might be translated in modern terms as 'Total War'. This was the form of war waged by Christendom against the infidels and it permitted both the slaughter and enslavement of foes, whereas other forms of warfare were either more restrained or were simply illegal. The moral problems faced by a Christian knight during the 12th century were summed up by Stephen of Muret, who stated that a knight could not refuse

obedience to his secular lord but could absolve himself from evil while taking part in an evil enterprise by telling God that he wanted only to be a Christian knight and that he would 'seek after that which is good on every occasion as much as I can'.

By 1200 the attitudes of theologians and ecclesiastical lawyers were already diverging, with the latter accepting that what was lawful in time of peace was not necessarily the same as what was lawful in time of war, particularly religiously motivated war. There was also further development of St Augustine's idea that fighting 'evil' could be an act of love and that this could extend to the slaughter of infidels. According to the mid-12th-century lawyer Master Rolandus, for example, 'To kill evil persons for purposes of correction and justice is actually to minister unto God.' It was, in other words, a form of Christian charity to the wicked. Wars to defend the Holy Land were, therefore, both Just and Holy in the eyes of most medieval churchmen and lawyers.

The huge Hospitaller castle at Marqab, known to the crusaders as Margat, stands on a steep hill overlooking the Syrian coast and the town of Banyas, here marked by the tall chimneys of a modern power station. (David Nicolle)

A Brief History of the Hospitallers

OPPOSITE

*The area in the middle
of the Old City of
Jerusalem, immediately
south of the Church
of the Holy Sepulchre,
largely belonged to the
Order of Hospitallers in
the 12th century. After
Jerusalem was liberated
by Saladin in 1187,
however, the ancient
Mosque of the Caliph
Umar was rebuilt.
(David Nicolle)*

During the 11th century the terms 'hospital' and 'hospice' were sometimes interchangeable, meaning places where travellers could find shelter and support if sick, though very little in terms of medical treatment. Such hospitals were almost invariably attached to a church or run by people attached to a church because the Church was the only organization capable of undertaking such responsibilities.

The establishment of such hospitals for pilgrims and poor travellers was a feature of the 11th and 12th centuries and was seen across much of Europe. One group of Amalfitan merchants took charge of a hospice for Western European pilgrims in Jerusalem some time before 1071. It was a relatively new foundation replacing an earlier hospice in the Benedictine Monastery of Sancta Maria Latina (St Mary of the Latins) near the Church of the Holy Sepulchre. A female hospice was established a little further south in 1081–82, followed by a third Amalfitan hospice founded for men only. This was again dependent upon the church of Sancta Maria Latina and stood just west of the church of Sancta Maria Magdalena.

Unlike most of the other Latin hospitals in the Islamic Middle East, that established by the Amalfi merchants in Jerusalem lasted for a long time and became so popular that it attracted much of the Latin Catholic congregation away from the Greek Orthodox-dominated church of the Holy Sepulchre. The others seem to have failed because of a lack of support. Before the First Crusade erupted across the Holy Land a few years later, sick men and women were tended in these hospices by people who followed a quasi-religious way of life but do not seem to have been members of a recognized religious order. A man named Gerard was probably their guardian and he was permitted by the Fatimid Muslim governor to remain in Jerusalem during the crusaders' savage assault upon that city; virtually all the other Christians had been expelled for security reasons.

The supposed skull of the Blessed Gerard, the first Master of the Order of Hospitallers, is preserved as one of the Order's most sacred relics.(J. Azzopardi, The Order's Early Legacy in Malta, *Malta, Said International Ltd, 1989)*

Not surprisingly, legends later arose around Gerard, not least because his small hospice was the seed from which the Order of Hospitallers grew. This hospital was separated from Sancta Maria Latina after the crusader conquest but was not placed under the control of the Church of the Holy Sepulchre. Instead it was distanced from the latter's authority by a special papal privilege in 1113, and with the peaceful Blessed Gerard being claimed as the Military Order's first Master. As such it remained autonomous, unlike comparable hospitals in Western Europe.

A few years later the hospital in Jerusalem became fully independent when its Master obtained papal exemption from obedience to the Patriarch of Jerusalem, who was the senior churchman in the crusader kingdom. This caused anger and bitterness within the established Church hierarchy of the Crusader States, though initially the hospital in Jerusalem was not alone in enjoying a privileged position. Two other hospitals had been founded after the First Crusade in the County of Tripoli, one at the church of St John the Baptist near Mont Pélerin and another at Rafaniyah, but these lost their independence in 1126 when they were placed under the Order of the Hospitallers.

Other hospitals were attached to the major Orthodox churches in the Crusader States and neighbouring areas, including the great monastery of St Catherine beneath Mount Sinai, which had its own secondary hospital in Jerusalem. During the 13th century yet others were established in the crusader kingdom of Cyprus and the short-lived Latin Empire of Constantinople, although most were eventually taken over by the Hospitallers.

The Hospitallers may have acquired the ex-Greek Orthodox church of St John the Baptist immediately after the crusader conquest, although the date is unclear, and even while Gerard was still in charge the hospice evolved into a flourishing institution with wide support and considerably extended buildings. Gerard himself died in 1120, by which time the institution was already effectively independent of other Church structures within the kingdom. It also seems likely that the first Templars lived in these Hospitaller quarters and that their brotherhood was established under Hospitaller influence. The original hospital had been created under the supervision of the Benedictine monastic order before the arrival of the First Crusade, but was separated from the Benedictines soon after the conquest of Jerusalem.

THE TRANSITION FROM HOSPICE TO MILITARY ORDER

The process by which the charitable and medical Hospital of St John in Jerusalem took on a military character is not entirely clear. After the Kingdom of Jerusalem was established in 1100, the brethren of the hospital in Jerusalem gradually became more French and less Italian, and more militarized as the peaceful heritage of their Amalfitan founders faded. The success of the First Crusade had largely been a result of superior numbers, cohesion and motivation at a time when the Islamic lands of the Middle East were in a state of singular disunity, both political and religious, which in several areas verged upon fragmentation if not outright anarchy. These were circumstances that were never repeated, and no subsequent crusade enjoyed the success of the first.

However, once the majority of the participants had gone home, the new Crusader States that had been established in the Middle East found themselves in a position of acute manpower shortage. It soon became clear that some sort of standing force was required to protect the Western European, Latin Catholic pilgrims who were frequently attacked by bandits or raiders in the hills between the coast and Jerusalem and the river Jordan. At this time Palestine possessed

OPPOSITE

The papal bull, or letter of authorization, from Pope Paschal II confirming the foundation of the Order is perhaps the Hospitallers' most valued document. (Armoury of the Knights of St John, Valetta, Malta; G.F. Laking)

very few fortifications other than those of the main towns and a few small refuges for merchant caravans along the main roads.

The results were the newly formed Order of the Templars and the newly militarized Order of Hospitallers. A direct link between these first Christian Military Orders and the Islamic system of *ribats*, where Muslim volunteers spent short or extended periods in prayer and military service, defending the frontiers of the Islamic world, has been suggested but there seem to have been no such ribats in the Middle East at the time of the First Crusade and the appearance of the Military Orders a few years later. Though they did exist in al-Andalus, the Islamic regions of what are now Spain and Portugal, where they may have had some influence upon the emergence of the temporary confraternities who preceded the Iberian Military Orders, that was surely too far away to have any direct bearing upon events in Syria and Palestine.

The Hospitallers' first castle was probably that of Calansue (Qalansuwa) on the coastal plain between Caesarea and Arsuf, which was donated to the Order by a local crusader lord, Geoffrey de Flugeac, in 1128. The strategic castle of Bayt Jibrin in the foothills between Ascalon and the Dead Sea was given to the Order in the mid-1130s by King Fulk of Jerusalem, as were several grants of land in the Principality of Antioch, on condition they were fortified. This cannot be taken as proof of the militarization of the Order, because fortresses may have been garrisoned by paid retainers of the Hospital, but other evidence does suggest that the Order was assembling a military force.

The Order's involvement in a division of spoils with the Count of Tripoli in 1142–44 does seem to imply some military role, as did the right, allowed by the rulers of the Crusader States, to make truces with the Muslims without the Count of Tripoli's expressed approval. Hospitaller property in Tripoli consisted of a virtually autonomous enclave in the north-east of the country. This was based upon the fertile Buqai'ah valley between Mount Lebanon and the Syrian coastal mountains. Since this valley was the only practical link for large armies and major trading purposes between the Mediterranean coast and the great Islamic cities of the Syrian interior, it was also strategically sensitive. The Hospitallers put considerable effort into developing, controlling and defending this strategic 'Buqai'ah gap'. Though fertile and with enough rainfall to sustain year-round agriculture, it lacked natural defences and was very exposed to Muslim attack, most notably from the strongly fortified city of Homs. Under such circumstances it is hardly surprising that the main fortress of the area, Crac des Chevaliers, which was built upon the earlier Arab castle of Hisn al-Akra, became what is now widely recognized as the finest castle in the world. Nor were the Hospitallers' efforts in vain, since their palatinate (territory whose feudal lord effectively had sovereign authority) was the only significant region south of

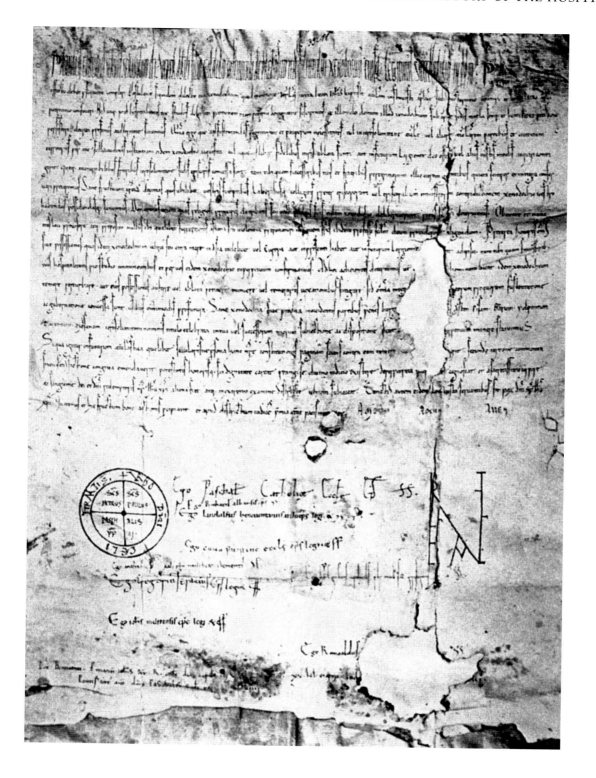

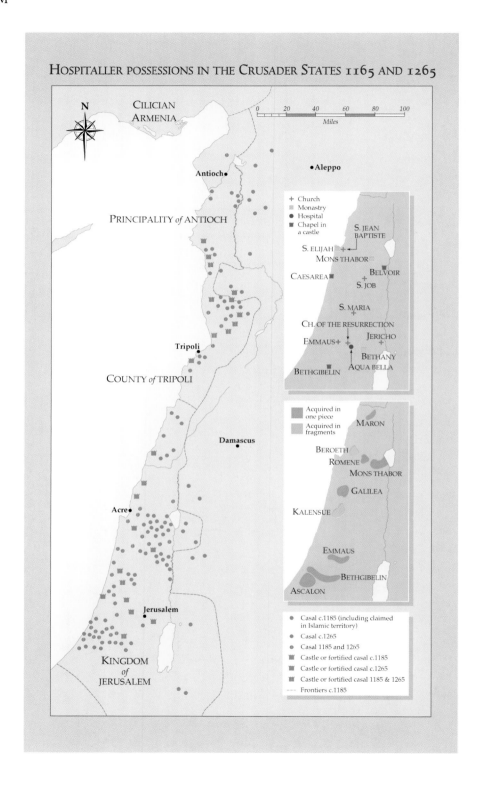

Pilgrims or other travellers on a 13th-century carved capital in southern France. (in situ, church of St Just, Valcabrere, France; David Nicolle)

the Principality of Antioch that Saladin failed to recapture after his great victory at Hattin in 1187. Other territory which was handed to the Hospitallers near this strategic enclave included the castle at Jabal Akkar, which they only held for a short while, and the castle of Castel Rouge for which the Montolieu family, its previous owners, received 400 bezants (a coinage based upon that of the Byzantine Empire) in compensation.

Despite the grants of such lands and privileges, it is not entirely clear when the Hospitallers first took on a fighting role. Documents from 1136 to 1143 mention arms and horses being donated to the hospitals in France and Spain, though these might again have been for servants of the Order rather than the brethren themselves. Also in the mid-12th century in the Iberian peninsula, the Military Orders started playing a significant role in what is now known as the Reconquista. Here the Hospitallers also appeared on the scene before the Templars. At first they were confined to a non-military role but in 1149 Hospitallers were given the castle of Amposta near Tortosa, after they had taken part in the siege of that city.

Knightly volunteers seem unlikely to have attached themselves to the Hospitallers unless it already included a military force but it was not until 1182, by which time the Crusader States were already seriously short of military manpower, that there is the first undeniable reference to Hospitaller brethren themselves including military personnel.

In 1186, the Hospitallers acquired the castle of Marqab, which was perhaps even more dramatic than Crac des Chevaliers and which overlooked the coast north-west of Crac. The original castle was sold to the Order by the Mazoir family, a dynasty that came from southern France and was one of the last of the great feudatories of the Crusader States to sell its main castle to the Military Orders. In return the Mazoirs received an annual pension of 2,200 gold coins to be paid in Tripoli. Titles to several other lesser castles were also acquired by the Hospitallers in this region, though some of them were already in Muslim hands. Others, like Qadmus in the Syrian mountains, were shortly lost to the Isma'ilis – popularly, though inaccurately, known as Assassins.

Meanwhile the Hospitallers' Templar rivals were busy creating a comparable autonomous palatinate around Tarsus just south of Marqab. At the same time, the Crusader States' failure to expand inland or towards Egypt, followed by a dramatic loss of land to Muslim reconquest, then forced them to maintain large defensive armies while lacking sufficient land to support such armies in the normal feudal manner. Consequently the Crusader States soon consisted of largely urban coastal populations that had more in common with Italy than with France. They were also obliged to rely increasingly upon the Military Orders and hired mercenaries to provide adequate military forces.

For the Hospitallers, the most significant event in the latter part of the 12th century was the kingdom's loss of Jerusalem itself and most of its other territory to Saladin. After the Third Crusade recovered Acre, the Hospitallers' main convent or headquarters was re-established there. From now on the nominal Kingdom of Jerusalem, like the other Crusader States, concentrated upon preserving what it had, with few attempts to take additional territory. Even when Jerusalem was briefly returned to crusader hands by treaty between 1229 and 1244 the Hospitaller convent remained in Acre, though the Order did retake possession of its old buildings. Meanwhile the Holy Land itself had become a sort of huge holy relic to be preserved from the infidels.

During the 13th century the Hospitallers, the Templars and the more recently created Order of Teutonic Knights took control of an increasing number of key crusader fortresses. The huge cost of maintaining, strengthening and garrisoning such places was best borne by the increasingly wealthy Military Orders. At the same time, the aristocratic families of the Crusader States were falling upon hard times, losing the estates whose revenues were essential to pay the costs of castles. Steady territorial gains by the Mamluk Sultanate, which soon virtually surrounded the enfeebled Crusader States on land, ruined many such settler families, who therefore sold their *casals* or farms, perhaps including titles to those estates already lost to the Muslims, sometimes to repay their debts to the Military Orders.

Even within the by now crowded and greatly expanded city of Acre there seems to have been plenty of property for sale as people tried to sell up and leave the doomed crusader enclaves. By the 1280s the Hospitallers and other Military Orders saw themselves as the real if not the legal rulers of what remained of the

Christian-ruled Holy Land. This reality is clear in legal and diplomatic documents, such as the 1283 Treaty of Truce between the Kingdom of Jerusalem – now consisting of little more than Acre itself – and the neighbouring Mamluk Sultanate. It is counter-signed by the Masters of the Hospitallers, Templars and Teutonic Knights, amongst others.

THE HOSPITALLERS IN THE CHRISTIAN STATES

In the Iberian peninsula, however, the Christian states were expanding rather than retreating, and although the Hospitallers' largest pool of financial resources lay within the heartlands of Western Catholic Christendom, the Order did receive booty and tribute from Iberian frontier regions. In the early 13th century, in the immediate aftermath of the Fourth Crusade, the Military Orders were also offered substantial estates within the still unconquered Anatolian regions of the Byzantine Empire. In the event, the Western crusaders never did take control of much of Anatolia and even within those limited provinces where the Latin Empire did briefly rule, the Templars seem to have been more powerful than the Hospitallers. It is possible that the Hospitallers had a small role in the conquest of Greece, where longer-lasting though never particularly powerful Crusader States were established in the wake of the Fourth Crusade's conquest of Constantinople in 1204.

Another region where the Hospitallers clearly maintained a brief military presence was in the huge kingdom of Hungary. Here, in 1247, King Bela IV granted them the Severin area in what is now south-western Romania, plus rights over unconquered Kipchaq-held areas to the east. In return the Hospitallers promised to help fight all pagans (Cumans or Kipchaq Turks) and schismatics (Bulgarians).

This agreement was confirmed by the Pope four years later but there is no evidence that the Hospitallers either helped defend Hungary against the first Mongol invasion in 1248, or defended Severin when this was again raided by the Mongols in 1260. The only real result was the steady feudalization of regions which had until then retained traditional, almost tribal forms of socio-political organization. The area to the west of the River Olt remained largely traditional, consisting of various *knezats* and *voivodates* (types of territorial governorates and their rulers) ruled by an indigenous aristocracy, and was effectively independent of Hospitaller authority. While the local knezeats and voivodates already had their own troops, the towns and small number of stone fortifications that now began to appear largely did so as a result of Hungarian and Hospitaller influence. In fact, the voivode of Curtea de Arges eventually became the Grand Voivode and was recognized outside the region as the Prince of Wallachia. By 1320 his principality was expanding towards the Black Sea coast and a generation or so later the Hospitallers would return to this area as part of the disastrous Crusade of Nicopolis in which a future prince of Wallachia played a prominent role.

THE HOSPITALLERS AFTER THE FALL OF ACRE

The fall of Acre to the Mamluks in 1291, followed by the immediate surrender or evacuation of the remaining crusader coastal enclaves, was a catastrophe for the Military Orders in the Middle East. It eventually proved fatal for the Templars, though the Hospitallers weathered the storm and emerged stronger than before, as they were granted properties that had formerly belonged to the Templars. In practice, it sometimes cost the Hospitallers considerable sums of money before they were able to take real control of ex-Templar estates that the Pope had transferred to them. In Germany, for example, the Order had to pay the powerful Margrave of Brandenburg the equivalent of 310 kilograms of silver before he finally handed over the Templar properties in his area in 1318.

With the loss of Acre, the Hospitallers re-established their convent on the island of Cyprus. Then came a prolonged period of reorganization and a gradual refocussing of the Order's military efforts upon naval warfare. However, Cyprus did not prove suitable as a headquarters. There was tension between the Order and the king of Cyprus, the kingdom was unstable and the island itself lacked sufficient available resources. For a while the Armenian Kingdom of Cilicia was

Knights jousting was a very popular subject across most of Western and Central Europe during the 12th century. Here in Navarre, in northern Spain, they are joined by a third warrior, slaying a serpent with his spear and bearing a cross upon his shield.(in situ, parish church, Artaiz, Spain; David Nicolle)

'Siege of Antioch', Histoire Universelle, Crusader States. Though illustrating an episode from the First Crusade, the Christian warriors in the lower register of this decorated initial are dressed and armed in the style of the second half of the 13th century when the manuscript was made, possibly in Antioch itself. (f.40r, M.S. Pal. Lat. 1963, Vatican Library, Rome, Italy)

considered as an alternative location but was too weak and vulnerable. Although this Armenian kingdom had in many respects evolved into a 'Crusader State' on the Middle Eastern mainland, having a long tradition of close military and political relations with the Hospitallers, it was still not a 'Latin' or Western European Christian realm.

The most immediate problem for the Hospitallers had been the loss of many of the Order's most experienced brethren at the fall of Acre. The Grand Master, Jean de Villiers, survived but was severely wounded. Vital archives and documentation, not to mention several important sources of revenue, had also been lost. In fact the Military Orders had not only failed in their primary task of defending the Kingdom of Jerusalem but, in the eyes of many, had lost their reason for existence because they were no longer able to protect pilgrims in the Holy Land. The Hospitallers promptly set about establishing a new hospital in Limassol but as yet there was little more that they could do other than join other Latin forces in preparation for an expected Mamluk invasion of Cyprus.

In the event this threat did not materialize. Instead, Cyprus was flooded with refugees, many of whom had arrived even before Acre fell. Many of the mainland coastal towns had been lost before Acre and it seems that the majority of survivors from these crusader enclaves came from what had been the Principality of Antioch and the County of Tripoli. Others had fled to Armenian Cilicia though most of these refugees appear to have been merchants rather than members of a now landless aristocracy. Some fled further, to Italy. Many families in the Latin States had recognized that they had no future in the Middle East following previous Mamluk successes, but only those with ready cash could escape. They included the prosperous peasantry but not the rural and urban poor, who had to remain.

Once Jean de Villiers was sufficiently recovered, the Hospitaller survivors from Acre held a Chapter General or meeting in Cyprus. The Pope agreed that Limassol would be the Order's new headquarters and in 1292 he authorized the Master to use the Order's small fleet of galleys to defend Armenian Cilicia. The Pope had already ordered the Hospitallers to increase the size of their fleet. Unfortunately the naval situation was soon complicated by a bitter war between the Italian merchant republics of Genoa and Venice, both of which were in naval terms hugely more powerful than the Hospitallers, and who carried their war to the eastern Mediterranean.

Under such circumstances it is hardly surprising that a new Master of the Hospitallers, Guillaume de Villaret, wanted to transfer the Order's headquarters to Provence in southern France, but this was resisted by the brethren in Cyprus who threatened to revolt. Meanwhile the papacy itself was involved in quarrels nearer home, enthusiasm for crusading was dwindling and the shadow of dissolution was soon hanging over the Templars. For its part, the leadership of the Hospitallers fluctuated between vague schemes to attack Mamluk Egypt or Syria, or to move to Cilicia, or to move to the now revived Byzantine Empire. Many in the Order of Hospitallers seemed reluctant to act at all, being almost paralysed by recent catastrophes and current difficulties. Numerous impractical schemes for new crusades were conjured up in Western Europe, most of them expecting the Military Orders to take a leading role that their current weaknesses made impossible. Others suggested, perhaps more realistically, that the Hospitallers and Templars be united into one great Crusading Order, though nothing ever came of this idea. In 1305 the Masters of these two Orders both favoured an attack upon Egypt, to be launched from Cyprus. In the meantime the Hospitallers sent two expeditions to Armenian Cilicia and took part in coastal raids against both Egypt and Syria.

The fall of the tiny Templar-held island of Ruad, just a kilometre off the Syrian coast facing Tartus, as well as the Mamluk defeat of the Mongols followed by the latter's conversion to Islam, effectively marked the end of crusader attempts to retake the Holy Land using Cyprus as a naval base. Cyprus did however remain a launching pad for piratical raids against the Islamic coasts and to support the declining Kingdom of Armenian Cilicia. The Hospitallers contributed to both these endeavours and, by the early 14th century, the Order was formally established in western Cilicia, on what is now the southern coast of Turkey. Here its primary role was to defend Armenian Cilicia against Turkish raids from the interior. However, Cilicia had few harbours and an unhealthy coast that was already dominated by Italian merchants. In addition to being vulnerable to Turkish raids, it was uncomfortably close to the regional superpowers of Mamluk Syria–Egypt and Mongol Iraq–Iran.

Morale was meanwhile shockingly low within the Order of Hospitallers, with reports of troops getting drunk and widespread indiscipline, at least amongst the Order's hired mercenaries. In addition, relations with King Henry II of Cyprus were strained. Henry still feared the Order's gradually reviving power and he tried to limit its importation of military supplies and acquisition of land. As a result the Hospitallers' estates on Cyprus were not sufficient to maintain their own people on the island. Instead the Order was dependent upon supplies from the West, mostly from the Angevin Kingdom of Naples in southern Italy. Consequently the Hospitallers limited their forces in the east and instead focussed upon strengthening their fleet. In this they were helped by a papal 'licence to arm shipping' in Cyprus without permission from the Cypriot ruler, which can hardly have improved relations between the Hospitallers and the king.

When Foulques de Villaret was elected Master of the Hospitallers in 1305 the Order entered a more active phase, particularly in naval warfare against the Mamluk Sultanate of Egypt. As already stated, Foulques de Villaret and the Master of the Templars both favoured an attack on Egypt using Cyprus as a base, while Pope Clement V clearly had a high opinion of the Masters' crusading expertise. Unfortunately the leaders of the two Orders had differing opinions. Both wrote reports, outlining what they regarded as the best way of regaining the Holy Land, but whereas the Templar memorandum was overconfident and even cocky in tone, that by Foulques de Villaret was very different. Longer, more carefully argued, less direct and more subtle, it read like a bureaucrat's report rather than one written by a military leader.

Foulques emphasized prudence and careful preparation, hinting that a series of small-scale operations over a prolonged period by professional and if necessary mercenary forces would be more effective in wearing down Mamluk power than the all-out crusading invasion which had so often come to grief in the past. The widest possible support should be sought, including alliances not only with the Christian Armenian Kingdom of Cilicia but also with the Mongols, though this

*A 12th-century
carved ivory or bone
backgammon piece
decorated with a knight riding
a cockerel. The style of helmet,
with a nasal piece that broadens
to form an almost complete face-
mask, strongly suggests that it
was made in the Christian
northern part of the Iberian
peninsula. Similar helmets
appear in Spanish manuscripts
and stone carvings but are
virtually unknown elsewhere
in 12th-century Europe.
(Musée Médiéval, Paris;
David Nicolle)*

broad strategic vision was now out of date as the Mongols were themselves in the process of converting to Islam. Above all there was the question of ensuring adequate finances for any new crusades.

How far Foulques de Villaret's ideas reflected the attitudes of the Hospitallers as a whole is unclear. Yet they suggest that the Order of Hospitallers, under his Mastership, was now an organization that was willing to lower its idealistic sights in order to accommodate current realities. Such realism probably prompted the Hospitallers to conquer the Byzantine island of Rhodes, which was even further from their Mamluk foes than was Cyprus. This campaign would also provide the Order with its own independent base – something which the Teutonic Knights were already establishing in the Baltic and which the doomed Templars never achieved. The conquest of Rhodes had formed part of an earlier but aborted idea of re-establishing the Latin Empire of Constantinople, lost to Byzantine reconquest in 1261.

THE HOSPITALLERS IN RHODES

The Hospitaller invasion of Rhodes began in 1306. The island had long been a fief of Genoese admirals in Byzantine service and the piracy that had been endemic through the Aegean for a century had grown worse after the Byzantines regained many of the islands. Meanwhile Western merchants and pirates were active around Rhodes, which Venice, as ruler of nearby Crete, also coveted. The Turks, who had reached the Aegean coast around 1302–03, may now have been trying to make the pirate-infested offshore islands a depopulated no-man's-land along their new maritime frontier. This was a long-established Islamic strategy and the Turkish rulers involved would undoubtedly have regarded the emergence of a warlike new Hospitaller state within this zone as a dangerous threat, especially as some Turkish forces were already operating on Rhodes.

One way or another, the Hospitallers were entering a chaotic region and found themselves up against two enemies: Muslim Turks and Orthodox Christian Byzantine Greeks whom the Hospitallers, as Latin Catholic Christians, regarded as schismatics. In the event it took the Order at least three years to take control of Rhodes, whereupon, according to a slightly later account of the conquest:

The Grand Master Foulques de Villaret and the valiant Brothers of the Hospital gave thanks to God and to the Virgin Mary for the wealth and abundance which had come to them. They built a great castle and conquered all around, collecting many fine men who wished to come to Rhodes to reconnoitre and to colonize the island. Then they had many places in Anatolia submit to their authority which gave them tribute.

The occupation of Rhodes provided the Order of Hospitallers with a new, secure location for its headquarters. The Hospitallers already had some property in what remained of the Crusader States of Greece, established in the aftermath of the Fourth Crusade, but although their possession of Rhodes and some smaller neighbouring islands gave them a secure and independent base, their military activity remained limited for several years. Foulques de Villaret started to behave like a despotic sovereign rather than an elected leader, which provoked a rebellion by many Hospitaller brethren in 1317. This crisis was only solved after the Pope intervened, Foulques de Villaret resigned and a new Master, Hélion de Villeneuve, took over. Now the Order began to take on a new role.

For many years the Hospitaller leadership had been arguing for a trade blockade of Egypt and their possession of Rhodes might now enable them and their crusading allies to put such a blockade in place. It also seems clear that, during the early 14th century, the Hospitallers still saw their traditional enemy, the powerful Mamluk Sultanate in Egypt and Syria, as the main target. Consequently, Hospitaller Rhodes developed into a centre for piracy or privateering rather than crusades in the traditional sense and, as Latin Crusader territory shrank elsewhere in Greece and the Aegean, so the strategic importance of Rhodes increased.

The Hospitaller Order itself became more powerful in Greece, as it did elsewhere, when the Hospitallers' great rival, the Order of the Templars, was dissolved in 1312 and its leaders executed as supposed heretics. It acquired ex-Templar property in the Morea (Peloponnese) and Crete, though the Templars' other estates in central Greece went to a secular lord, Walter of Châtillon. This may have been because the Hospitallers were already very selective when it came to taking on responsibility for new territories, particularly those in exposed locations like central Greece, which needed to be defended. Additionally, it is clear that the south-eastern Aegean was now the Order's priority, as it remained until the fall of Rhodes in 1522.

In strategic and naval terms, Rhodes dominated several hundred miles of the Anatolian or Turkish coast. During the 1320s the nearby Turkish *emirate* or *beylik* (Arabic and Turkish terms for a small state or independent territory) of Mentese was virtually denied access to the sea and so the main centre of Turkish naval operations shifted northwards to the beylik of Aydin. As yet this lay beyond the Hospitallers' immediate zone of operations and so flotillas of small Turkish raiding ships from Aydin dominated much of the Aegean for several years. Although the Hospitallers' efforts to carve out a presence on the Anatolian mainland failed, several other small islands were seized, ranging from Lerro (now Léros) in the north to Castelrosso (now Kastellórizon) in the east. Scarpanto (now Kárpathos) in the west was, meanwhile, handed over to the Venetian governor of Crete.

In 1344 the Hospitallers joined other crusaders in seizing Aydin's main port of Smyrna (now Izmir), so the focus of Turkish naval operations shifted northwards yet again and ten years later the rapidly expanding Ottoman emirate, or sultanate as it soon became, crossed the Dardanelles and captured its first toe-hold on the European mainland on the Gallipoli peninsula. Rhodes remained secure, an island in seas that were still largely controlled by Christians. It was large, reasonably fertile and was located on the vital trade-route from the Black Sea to Egypt. This shipping lane not only supplied the Mamluk Sultanate with wood and iron but with the largely Turkish, nominally enslaved recruits who, once trained and freed, became the backbone of the Mamluk army and state.

Eventually strategic realities meant that there was a fundamental shift in the Hospitallers' military thinking, away from the eastern Mediterranean to the Aegean Sea. In military terms, Rhodes and the south-eastern Aegean remained the Hospitallers' primary consideration. On land there was very little fighting against the Turks during the late 14th and early 15th centuries, except for skirmishes referred to as *scaramuce*, most of which merely provoked enemy retaliation and were stopped in 1409. Thereafter the Latin powers in the Aegean region and Greece were too weak effectively to help the now rapidly declining Byzantine Empire, even if they felt inclined to do so.

Things were, meanwhile, changing on the Turkish side and by the 15th century the naval power of Mentese and Aydin was a thing of the past. Instead, following their conquest of the old Byzantine imperial capital of Constantinople (Istanbul) in 1453, the Ottoman Turks were soon bidding to dominate not only the Aegean but the entire eastern Mediterranean, the Balkans, the Middle East and North Africa. The Hospitallers were facing a rising superpower.

Despite occasional conflicts, the Mamluks and Hospitallers had, since the end of the 14th century, formed a strange, unofficial and perhaps uneasy alliance. Then, in 1517, 64 years after they conquered Byzantine Constantinople, the Ottomans overthrew the long-established and once powerful Mamluk Sultanate. Not only did the Hospitallers lose a potential ally, but the Ottomans now held the entire eastern Mediterranean coast as well as virtually all of Greece and most of the Balkans. Henceforth the Hospitallers were alone, except for the Venetians whose policy was to maintain peaceful trade with the Ottoman Empire whenever

Knights of St John going to war in a decorated initial in a 14th-century Spanish manuscript entitled Libro de los fechos et conquistas del principado de la Morea *of Grand Master Juan Fernandez de Heredia. (MS. 10.131, Biblioteca Nacional, Madrid, Spain)*

possible, and the Genoese who still clung to some islands north of Hospitaller territory. From the Ottoman Turkish point of view the continued existence of an aggressive crusader outpost straddling the vital sea lanes from Istanbul to the Ottomans' important new province of Egypt was intolerable.

Matters came to a head in 1522, with a second and this time successful Ottoman invasion of Rhodes. The Hospitallers finally left the island on 1 January 1523, after which the Master sailed first to Crete and then to the Papal States of

Central Italy. Latin churches throughout the ex-Hospitaller islands were converted to mosques and from that date until 1897 there were no Catholic residents in the fortified city of Rhodes. Although most of the Greek Orthodox population remained and transferred its allegiance to the Ottoman Sultan, some of the westernized Rhodian Greek elite chose to follow the Order into exile, a few eventually accompanying them to their new home on the island of Malta.

THE 16TH CENTURY: THE HOSPITALLERS AFTER RHODES

After the loss of Rhodes, the Hospitallers maintained a new headquarters in Viterbo in Italy for nearly four years, though they did have to move to Nice during an outbreak of plague in 1527. This was another period of great uncertainty for the Order, which found itself on the fringes of a bitter and prolonged war between France and Spain, as well as being uncomfortably close to Rome when it was sacked in the same year as the plague. Pope Clement VII tried to make the Hospitallers into a regiment of tame papal guards and for a while the Order seemed to be in danger of falling apart. Between 1522 and 1568 there was a series of important high-level meetings, known as Chapters General, which struggled to sort out the numerous problems concerning Hospitaller finances, administration and religious disputes. Not surprisingly, the eight years between the loss of Rhodes and the acquisition of a new home on Malta saw recruitment slump.

Once the Emperor Charles V had given Malta to the Order as its new and hopefully permanent home, the Hospitallers selected the fishing town of Birgu rather than the traditional Maltese inland capital of Mdina as their headquarters. They also set about strengthening the existing fortifications of Sant Angelo, overlooking Malta's main harbour. Between the move to Malta and the great siege of 1565 Hospitaller military operations were limited and not entirely successful. The world was changing fast around them and the medieval crusading ideal was becoming widely unfashionable. The Hospitallers' actions were particularly hampered by France, whose brief and supposedly 'Unholy Alliance' with the Ottoman Empire not only meant the end of French domination of the Order but sometimes resulted in French brother-knights taking part in joint Franco-Ottoman military or naval operations. Venice also remained hostile, regularly accusing the Hospitallers of piracy. Yet, wherever possible, the increasingly outdated Hospitallers of Malta carried on unrelenting privateering warfare against Ottoman shipping in the Aegean and other seas.

The Order also hoped to retake Rhodes, or at least to obtain a better base in Sicily. Tripoli in Libya (Trabulus al-Gharb or western Tripoli as distinct from Trabulus al-Sham or Syrian Tripoli) had been acquired at the same time as Malta

HOSPITALLER POSSESSIONS IN THE SOUTH-EASTERN AEGEAN C.1375

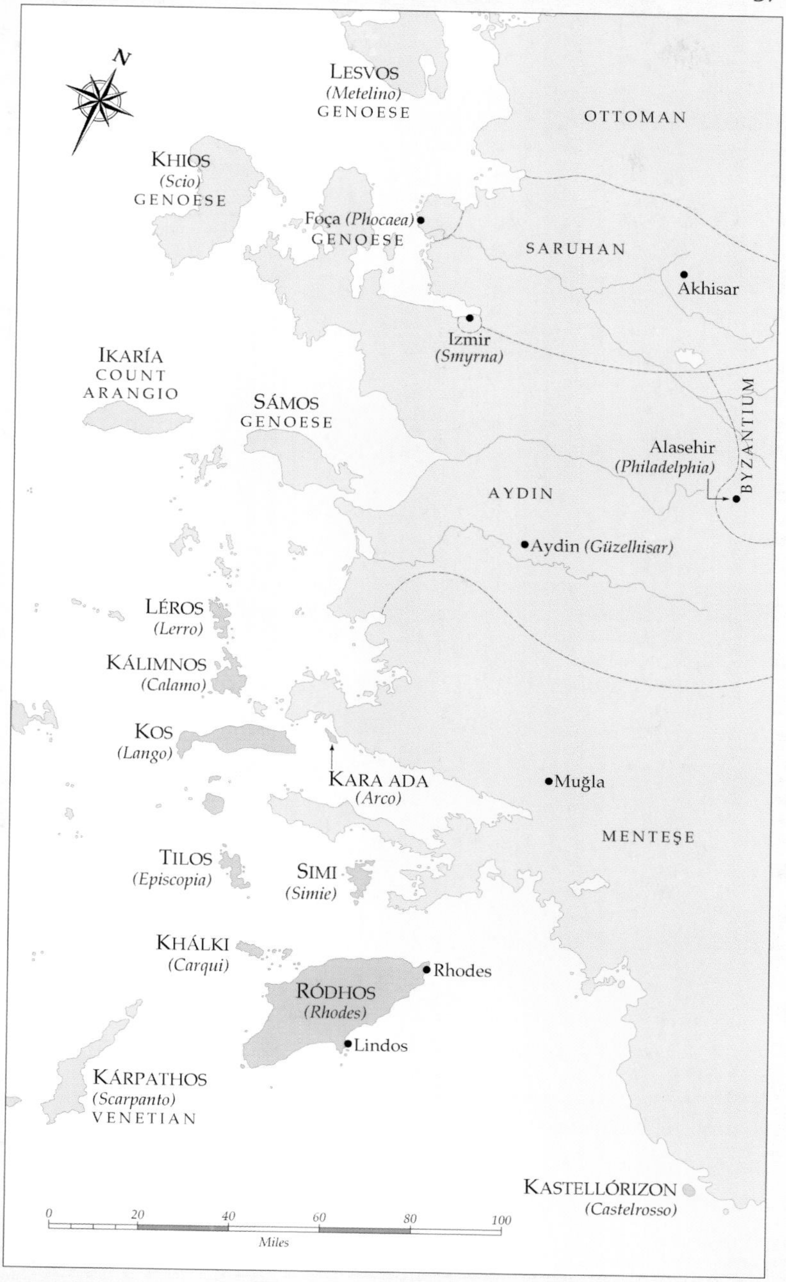

N

LESVOS
(Metelino)
GENOESE

OTTOMAN

KHIOS
(Scio)
GENOESE

Foça *(Phocaea)* ●
GENOESE

SARUHAN

● Akhisar

Izmir
(Smyrna)

IKARÍA
COUNT
ARANGIO

SÁMOS
GENOESE

BYZANTIUM

Alasehir
(Philadelphia)

AYDIN

● Aydin *(Güzelhisar)*

LÉROS
(Lerro)

KÁLIMNOS
(Calamo)

KOS
(Lango)

KARA ADA
(Arco)

● Muğla

MENTEŞE

TILOS
(Episcopia)

SIMI
(Simie)

KHÁLKI
(Carqui)

● Rhodes

RÓDHOS
(Rhodes)

● Lindos

KÁRPATHOS
(Scarpanto)
VENETIAN

KASTELLÓRIZON
(Castelrosso)

0   20   40   60   80   100
Miles

33

The cloisters of what was once the abbey church of St Mary of the Latins, the mother house or Hospitaller headquarters in Jerusalem. (D. Bahat)

but proved such a liability that its loss in 1551 came as a relief, enabling the Hospitallers to concentrate on strengthening Malta itself. Here improvements to the fortifications in and around Birgu were completed just in time for the great Ottoman assault of 1565.

The Englishman Richard Knolles in his *General Historie of the Turkes* published several decades later claimed to quote Sultan Sulayman's justification for this attack. Indeed Knolles apparently drew upon Ottoman sources via a French translation as well as other travellers to Istanbul. The sultan's words were remarkably similar to Venetian complaints about the Order when he described the Hospitaller brethren as 'Pirates bearing crosses which vaunt themselves to be the bulwark of Christendom'. Addressing his followers, Sultan Sulayman the Magnificent continued, 'You yourselves daily hear the pitiful complains of our subjects and merchants, whom these Maltese, I say not soldiers but pirates, if they but look into those seas, spoil and make prizes of, whose injuries to revenge all laws both of God and men do require.' The Ottoman Turks were wholly defeated in the ensuing siege. Whether this was the turning point in history that so many historians claim remains doubtful. It certainly did not destroy or even particularly damage Ottoman naval or military might. Nor did it change the course of Ottoman expansion. What the great siege of 1565 did do was to revive Hospitaller morale, prestige, recruitment and support within the Catholic Christian world. In some respect the siege of Malta was like an echo of the medieval past, and from that date onward the Hospitallers began to regain some strength and influence.

THE HOSPITALLERS AND THE POWERS OF LATIN CHRISTENDOM

The Hospitallers and the Popes

The most important power relationship in Hospitaller history was that between the Order and the papacy. Few things illustrate the autonomy of the Hospitallers better than the fact that popes were rarely confident of committed support from the Military Orders in their various quarrels with other powers in Latin Catholic Europe. During the crisis between the various popes and the German emperor, which dominated so much of later 12th-century European history, the Hospitallers had supported the papacy while many secular rulers supported the German emperor. This allegiance hindered the development of the Order of Hospitallers in Central and Eastern Europe and may have made the Masters of the Order wary of involvement in papal quarrels in the future. The Military Orders were asked not to support the Hohenstauffen Emperor of Germany, with whom the papacy was currently having a particularly bitter quarrel, in his efforts to revive and strengthen the Crusader Kingdom of Jerusalem in the 1220s to 1240s.

Comparable tensions had already been apparent during the early 13th-century crusade against the Albigensian 'heretics' in southern France, where the Hospitallers had traditionally maintained good relations with the counts of Toulouse. Unfortunately the latter were now effectively the protectors of the Albigensians. In practical terms, the Hospitallers had few brethren-in-arms in France and little military equipment for those who were stationed there. Around the same time, the Church also asked both the Hospitallers and the

Templars to help quell disturbances amongst fellow Christians in Cyprus. Later in the 13th century, the Pope threatened to send the Military Orders against Bohemond VII of Tripoli and nominally of Antioch, who was accused of seizing possessions belonging to the Bishop of Tripoli.

The popes had learned at an early date to be wary of involving the Military Orders directly in their own political quarrels within Catholic Christendom, fearing accusations that this would divert the Orders' resources from the main struggle against the Muslims in and around the Holy Land. Instead, the papacy seems to have preferred to establish new, though rarely very successful, Military Orders to combat its foes within Italy. Although some Hospitallers were employed in papal service or in the Pope's military retinue, it was normally as individuals rather than as representatives of their Order. For example, the Pope seemed unwilling to use resident Hospitallers or Templars against the Aragonese who evicted his Angevin French allies from Sicily and threatened to overthrow the Angevin kingdom in southern Italy. Instead, brethren-in-arms in certain areas of conflict were asked to surrender their castles to the king of France, but not actively to take part in the fighting. This was despite several efforts by the papacy to equate its foes in southern Italy with Muslims or to condemn them as friends of Muslims. Even though the Hospitallers were not called upon to take part in these quarrels, the papacy still came under severe criticism both inside and outside the Church for diverting the resources at a time when the Crusader States in the Middle East and the Aegean were in danger of being overrun.

The papacy had greater influence, though still not control, over the Hospitaller Order during the 14th and 15th centuries. Though this freed the Hospitallers from much interference by secular rulers, it meant increased papal meddling in the day-to-day administration of the Order. In return, Hospitallers became increasingly prominent figures within the papal court, being sent as mediators to various European conflicts including the Hundred Years' War. Around 1340 they were even administering all the papal territories in central Italy on behalf of the absentee Pope, who was residing in Avignon because of a schism within the papacy.

The close relationship with the papacy meant that the Great Schism (1378–1417), in which rival popes held court in Rome and Avignon, was not only a scandal but a serious threat to Hospitaller unity. It is therefore a tribute to the dedication of the Hospitallers and the political skills of their leaders that the Order not only survived but played its part in ending the schism. The Hospitaller Master Philibert de Naillac took a leading role in the Council of Pisa, which deposed both rival popes and elected a third in 1409. When the Schism officially ended it was de Naillac who actually crowned the now universally recognized Pope Martin V.

The Hospitallers' loss of Rhodes in 1522 again made the Order vulnerable to papal interference. Once its headquarters had settled in Italy the Hospitaller

*Archaeologists and art historians
have found that a greater number
of churches dating from the
crusader period survive in
Lebanon than was once thought.
Some also have fragments of
decoration but this example
is unusual in preserving
such extensive 13th-century
wall-paintings. (in situ,
parish church, Bahdeidat,
Lebanon; Erica Dodd)*

Master, Philippe Villiers de L'Isle Adam, was appointed Guardian of the Papal Conclave, which elected a new pope in 1523. He was Clement VII, himself a Knight of the Hospitaller Order and had formerly been Prior of Capua.

The Hospitallers and the Crusader States

The relationship between the Hospitallers and the Crusader States was in some ways more straightforward than their relations with the popes. The preservation of Christian control over the Holy Land was regarded as the responsibility of all Christendom, but it led to considerable outside interference in the affairs of the Kingdom of Jerusalem, and to a lesser extent of the other Middle Eastern Crusader States. Insubordination and divided leadership remained major problems for most crusading armies, even for that of the Kingdom of Jerusalem itself. Clearly defined feudal limitations of the military service that could be demanded of the European settler aristocracies in the Middle East similarly reduced the already limited military potential of these small realms.

The Orthodox church of Santa Spiridon in the old city of Rhodes dates from the 13th century. It survived the centuries of Hospitaller rule but was turned into a mosque following the Ottoman conquest and is currently disused. (David Nicolle)

The Crusader States of the Middle Eastern mainland were militarily and financially almost exhausted by the mid-12th century, a situation that resulted in increasing papal support for the Military Orders, which came to be seen as the most reliable and strongest military forces available for the defence of the Holy Land. The situation was further complicated by the emergence of what might be called a 'peace party' within the Crusader States during the second half of the 12th century. This party grew in influence amongst the settler aristocracy, including its knightly class, much of which wanted to achieve a peaceful accommodation with its Muslim neighbours. These settlers in turn were often accused of a lack of faith and even of cowardice by the local 'war party', which tended to be supported by newcomers from Western Europe.

During the 12th and much of the 13th century the Military Orders could be placed within the 'war party', though their approach was more sophisticated in practice. It is also clear that the Latin Catholic Church hierarchy within the Crusader States soon favoured strengthening the position of the Hospitallers and other Military Orders. Partly as a result of this support, the Hospitallers acquired many urban as well as rural possessions: not just the fortified walls and gates that they held in Sidon, Acre, Tripoli, Ascalon and Jaffa, but also ordinary houses, bakeries, mills, inns, markets and indeed properties relating to all aspects of economic life. In the countryside the Hospitallers soon owned extensive gardens, vineyards and uncultivated lands as well as an increasing number of castles.

It was the Hospitallers' acquisition of fortifications that above all increased their influence within government while reducing that of the settler aristocracy. Furthermore, their freedom of action was strengthened because the Military Orders did not normally owe feudal military service in return for their estates and castles. Instead these were held in *frankalmoign* – 'tenure in free alms', or in modern terms, freehold. The process of land acquisition could soon be seen in all the remaining Crusader States. In 1168, for example, Prince Bohemond III of Antioch gave the Hospitallers large tracts of land on both sides of the river Orontes, though much of this land was already back in Muslim hands and was never regained by the Hospitallers.

Despite its weakness and limited territory, the nominal Kingdom of Jerusalem remained rich. Consequently the Hospitallers and Templars were by no means the only wealthy sources of power in the area. It has been estimated that the annual revenues of the port-city of Acre alone were more than the annual revenue of the English crown during the mid-13th century. Most of Acre's wealth came from taxes levied on passing trade and although some of this was used to hire mercenaries, the permanent military establishment of the Crusader States was effectively controlled by the Military Orders, the urban merchant classes and groups of foreign merchants during much of the 13th century. At the same time the Hospitallers continued to acquire castles and estates. Nor were they obliged to maintain a specified number of troops in return for these lands. In contrast it was they who now called the shots, sometimes even insisting that they must have the right to keep any territory they won from Muslim neighbours before they would agree to take responsibility for a frontier fortress. Under such circumstances it is hardly surprising to find that the Hospitallers were able to make war upon their neighbours as and when they rather than the nominal government of the Crusader States saw fit.

The Latin Empire of Constantinople did not survive long enough to have many dealings with the Hospitallers, though even as early as 1205 Emperor Baldwin granted the Order a quarter of the Duchy of Navarino plus four fiefs in the Morea (Peloponnese). The land was to be used to raise money for the defence of the Holy Land but the Hospitallers were also required to defend these areas against 'schismatics', meaning the Byzantine Greeks.

Dealings between the Hospitallers and the kingdom of Cyprus were rather different. During the 13th century the Order had developed close relations with

Paradoxically, the best-preserved early or mid-13th century Christian wall paintings in what might be called a 'crusader style' are actually in a monastery church north-east of Damascus in an area that never fell under crusader domination. They are also strong evidence that the artists who decorated such religious buildings not only worked on both sides of the frontier but saw no problem in giving warrior saints, such as St Bacchus seen here, various items of typically Western European harness or military equipment. (in situ, monastery church of Mar Musa al-Habashi, Syria; David Nicolle)

the originally French Lusignan dynasty that ruled Cyprus. These ties deteriorated during the early 14th century, and, while the Templars faced increasing hostility and envy from the king of France, there was comparable if less dangerous tension between the Hospitallers and the king of Cyprus.

Relations with the powerful and hugely influential kingdom of France were extremely important for both Hospitallers and Templars. When the Templars were destroyed by King Philip of France for his own rather short-sighted purposes, the rival Hospitallers managed to maintain good, or at least adequate, relations with the powerful rulers of France. There was even some revival of enthusiasm for the crusade following a disastrous defeat by the Ottomans at the battle of Nicopolis in 1396, though it was largely concentrated in Burgundy and neighbouring regions. Such enthusiasm was clouded by romantic chivalric notions, which had little to do with military or political reality. Furthermore, the success of the kingdom of Hungary in containing the perceived threat of an Ottoman advance into Central Europe meant that papal calls for new crusades largely fell on deaf ears.

The Hospitallers and European Powers

King Henry II of England had been a keen supporter of crusading, though he never went on crusade himself, and on his death left a huge amount of money intended for the recruitment and payment of mercenaries for the Holy Land, including 5,000 marks each for the Hospitallers and Templars. Henry II's son, King Richard, became one of history's most famous crusaders, though not in reality a particularly successful one. In general, this tradition of support and occasional personal participation by England's princely elite continued throughout the 12th and most of the 13th century. However, there were also occasions when English rulers actively obstructed crusading as when, in 1275, King Edward I ordered the Hospitaller prior in Ireland not to travel east, though the latter had been ordered to do so by the Grand Master. In fact Edward threatened to confiscate Hospitaller lands if the prior left the country. English interest in the Hospitallers did increase following a visit to Rhodes by the Earl of Derby, who subsequently became King Henry IV, but in 1445 a meeting of the English *langue*, or basic linguistic division of the Order, in Rhodes was attended by only 11 brethren, five others being absent while one was on garrison duty in the subsidiary island of Lango (Kos).

Hospitaller relations with the German emperor were satisfactory, or at least stable, despite a natural tendency for German rulers to support their country's own Order of Teutonic Knights. One of the earliest references to what might have been a Hospitaller house in northern Europe was within the boundaries of the German Empire. This was a charter of 1122 listing imperial privileges to the cities of Utrecht and Muiden. It mentioned seven *Jerosolimitani*, ('of Jerusalem'),

Jokes and even mockery at the expense of the Military Orders became more widespread in the 13th and 14th centuries. Here the Masters of the Templars on the left, and of the Hospitallers on the right, are engaged in disputation supervised by the medieval chief of mischief and disrespect, Renart the Fox. (Jacquemart Giélée's Renart le Nouvel, *f.59, MS. Fr. 372, Bibliothèque Nationale de France, Paris)*

who may have been very early Hospitallers, invited to the city by its bishop. It thus seems possible that their hospital had already been established in Utrecht well before the Order was militarized, especially as the brethren in Utrecht were chaplains rather than knights. Thereafter there would continue to be more support for the Hospitallers than for the Templars in Germany and Eastern Europe, including Hungary, partly because the Templars were perceived as being too French and too close to the papacy.

Hospitaller relations with the fragmented powers of Italy were always complicated, even when the papacy is not considered. The Order's relationship with the Angevin rulers of southern Italy and Sicily, who also claimed the 13th-century crown of the crusader Kingdom of Jerusalem, was close. Here, following the Sicilian Vespers revolt in 1282, the Angevins decided that they could no longer afford to send troops to garrison Acre and therefore recalled their vicar or governor, Roger of San Severino, and his men. Roger was instead replaced as vicar and *bailli* by the seneschal or most senior military official of the Kingdom of Jerusalem, Odo of Poilechien, who largely relied upon on the Templars and the 'French Regiment', which was in turn maintained at French expense. Odo was forced to surrender the Citadel of Acre to the Angevins' rival as nominal ruler, King Henry of Cyprus. The Angevin King Charles II was in no position to reverse this collapse of power in the Holy Land, but he did confiscate some Hospitaller and Templar properties in Italy because the Orders had failed to support him in Acre.

If the Angevins' actions seemed vindictive, tensions between the Hospitallers and the powerful maritime Republic of Venice reflected their fundamentally different attitude towards dealings with the Islamic world. The Venetians were above all interested in trade. War remained a last resort, to be avoided wherever possible, be it against Muslims, schismatic Byzantines or fellow Catholics. These different attitudes and the resulting tensions long outlasted the Middle Ages and as a result very few Venetians joined the Order.

In contrast to Venice, the Hospitallers maintained reasonably friendly relations with Spain. In 1113 the Queen of Castile gave the village of Paradinas near Salamanca to the Hospitallers. Three years later another 11 villages were donated to the Order in the area of La Boveda de Toro, while the donation of the village of Atapuerca on the Pilgrim Road to Santiago by the queen's son enabled the Hospitallers to build a hospice for pilgrims. The Order was soon offering military protection as well, and in 1130 King Alfonso I of Aragon gave them the right to claim an annual dinner for two brethren travelling *cum suis armigeris*, 'with their squires'.

As already mentioned, the Hospitallers were present at the siege of Tortosa, and eight years later, in 1157, Count Raymond Berenguer IV 'The Saint' of Catalonia assigned one-tenth of all the land conquered from the Moors without foreign aid to the Order of Hospitallers.

RELATIONS WITH NON-LATINS AND NON-CHRISTIANS

Christians were still a majority in Syria and the northern Jazira (Mesopotamia) in the later 11th century and remained a substantial minority further south in Palestine. They were not, however, Latin Catholics. Instead, Jacobites or Syriac Christians and Armenians predominated in the north, with Orthodox Christians being more dominant in the south. In some parts of Egypt, meanwhile, indigenous Coptic Christians remained a majority. Within the Kingdom of Jerusalem itself one-third of the population may have consisted of European settlers, generally referred to as 'Franks', most of whom lived in towns or cities and were Latin Catholic Christians. Indigenous Christians and Muslims formed the other two-thirds, the great majority of whom were rural. There was also a significant Jewish minority. All the Muslims were from the lower social classes because the previous civil and military elites had been killed or expelled by the conquering crusaders.

The chapel in the Hospitaller castle of Marqab was at one time decorated with wall-paintings. Like the chapel at Crac des Chevaliers, it was converted into a mosque after the castle fell to the Mamluks. (David Nicolle)

As the territory of the Kingdom of Jerusalem shrank, however, so the proportion of Muslims decreased while that of Christians, both local and Latin, increased.

This was a complex and volatile environment for the Hospitallers, made increasingly difficult as relations between the Catholic and Orthodox Churches worsened in the later 12th century. After Saladin retook Jerusalem in 1187, most of the Latin churches were handed over to the Orthodox Christians.

Relations with the Armenians tended to be better, though they were not without problems. By the later 13th century the neighbouring Armenian Kingdom of Cilicia had become, in effect, a 'Crusader State' through its trade links with Western Europe, the significant role played by Military Orders in defence of its castles and by its strengthening links with the Kingdom of Cyprus.

The fact that the Hospitallers maintained reasonable relations with the Byzantine 'Empire of Nicaea' in the mid-13th century is remarkable given earlier tensions, an unofficial alliance between the Byzantine Empire and Saladin, and not least the Fourth Crusade's conquest and occupation of the Byzantine capital of Constantinople. The Order even obtained land and casals within what remained of Byzantine Anatolia during the reign of the Emperor John III Ducas Vatatzes. This led to tension between the Hospitallers and the then pope, Gregory IX, who wrote a letter of complaint to the Order: 'You are not ashamed to give aid against the Latins in horses and arms to Vatatzes'.

Elsewhere the Hospitallers occasionally found themselves involved in wars against Orthodox states such as Russia. Antagonism between Catholics and Orthodox Christians throughout Eastern Europe increased until, by the 14th century, some Westerners hated the 'Greeks' even more than the Muslims. This naturally made things more difficult for the Hospitallers once they were installed on Rhodes. The Aegean islands had been generally prosperous at the start of the 13th century, though their populations were already suffering from both 'Latin' piracy and Turkish raiding. In Rhodes itself the Hospitallers insisted that the local Orthodox Church recognize the supremacy of the Pope in Rome. Eventually most urban Greeks did so, and in 1437 the leader of the local Orthodox Church recognized the authority of the Pope, alongside the Catholic Archbishop. The rural Greek villagers apparently never accepted this state of affairs.

Relations between the Hospitallers and the local people of Rhodes were dominated by two factors. The first was the cultural and religious gulf between the Catholic Hospitallers and the Orthodox Greeks, which kept them apart. The second was the mutual concern for defence in a dangerous environment, which brought them together. This dichotomy was particularly obvious in the city of Rhodes where the local population had been expelled from the Old City, which was now reserved for the Hospitallers themselves. The indigenous Greeks were allocated a neighbouring suburb that had also been given a strong defensive wall by the mid-14th century. The different status of Greeks and Latins was similarly apparent in the size and value of the estates they were granted, those of Greeks being tiny while those of Latin settlers were sometimes large.

Mutual self-interest also lay behind the willingness of the Byzantine despot Theodore I of the Morea in southern Greece to sell the mighty fortress of Corinth to the Hospitallers in 1396, probably in the immediate aftermath of the Ottoman victory at Nicopolis over a crusade that included Hospitaller troops and ships. In contrast, many Greeks served in Turkish fleets during the 14th and 15th centuries, not only because they lived in areas now ruled by Turks but because hostility to the Latins, including the Hospitallers, ran so deep throughout the Aegean region. In the late 15th century Greeks from Rhodes itself were amongst those who urged the Ottoman Sultan Mehmet II, conqueror of the Byzantine imperial capital of Constantinople, to invade Rhodes. In yet another contrast that illustrated the complexity of the late medieval Aegean region, part of the Orthodox Greek elite in the city of Rhodes was by now so Westernized that when the Hospitallers finally surrendered to the Ottomans they chose to leave Rhodes with the Military Order in January 1523, some even following the Hospitallers to their new home in Malta.

Hospitaller relations with the Muslims were inevitably dominated by the ethos of the crusade, yet they were sometimes more complex than might be expected. The later 12th century had seen efforts by Western Latin Catholic Christian scholars to draw up a more careful refutation of Muslim beliefs, some scholars returning to an idea that had been current at the start of the relationship between Islam and Christianity: namely, that Islam was a form of heresy that nevertheless shared beliefs and values with Christianity. At the same time there was growing interest in the reality of Islamic civilization, not merely in myths and horror stories about supposedly barbarous 'pagans'. This change occurred at the same time as hostility towards Orthodox Byzantine civilization began to increase.

In more immediately practical terms, the rulers of the Crusader States, including the near-autonomous Hospitallers, did not enjoy complete control over many upland regions within their own claimed or nominal boundaries. Here the indigenous inhabitants, including those of substantially Muslim areas, were often virtually independent of outside interference, either from the Crusader States or from the Islamic cities of the interior. Elsewhere even unarmed villagers were able to exert some degree of independence when the power of their crusader rulers was in decline. For example, one Hospitaller document of 1263 bemoaned the fact that a Muslim village in Lower Galilee was refusing to pay its taxes to the Order because of waning Christian control over the area. Quite what the Hospitallers did on this occasion is unknown.

Some of the people of the Syrian coastal mountains had thrown off external domination at a much earlier date. The most dramatic and successful bid for independence was that by the Isma'ilis or so-called 'Assassins'. When the castle of Marqab was ceded to the Hospitallers in the late 12th century, its dependencies included Qadmus, 'Ullaiqa and Maniqa, all of which were already in Isma'ili hands. This situation seems to have been accepted by the Hospitallers, who presumably saw it as preferable to these mountain castles being in the hands of a major Muslim ruler. Thereafter the strength of the Hospitaller palatinate based upon Crac des Chevaliers meant that the Isma'ili statelet in the mountains to the north paid tribute to the Order in the mid-13th century. It has been suggested that the Isma'ilis also had some sort of military obligation to the Hospitallers and perhaps other crusader rulers as early as the mid- or late 12th century, though this seems unlikely. Instead the relationship seems almost to have been one of equals. In 1199, for example, the ruler of the Isma'ili mountain enclave opposed the transfer of the crusader castle of Maraclea, which had been destroyed by Saladin 11 years earlier, to the Hospitallers on the grounds that its dependency of Camel (Qalat al-Qsair) posed a threat to the major Isma'ili centres of Masyaf and al-Kahf. In the event the Hospitallers retained Maraclea and its substantial rents of 1,200 dinars (a coinage based on an Islamic prototype) plus 100 measures of wheat per year, until it fell to the Mamluk Sultan Baybars.

Sometimes the Isma'ilis found it difficult to pay their agreed tribute to the Hospitallers and Templars. In 1250–51 they even appealed for a reduction to King Louis IX of France when he arrived in Acre on crusade. In the event, their appeal failed and the Masters of the Military Orders threatened military reprisals if the Isma'ilis did not pay.

In the 12th century the Templars seem to have featured more prominently in Muslim views of the crusaders than did the Hospitallers. In his letter to the Caliph in Baghdad, announcing the great victory at Hattin in 1187, Saladin made specific mention of the Templars but not of the Hospitallers. Yet as Hospitaller power grew, so did their significance in the eyes of their enemies. Both Hospitallers and Templars had to negotiate truces with the increasingly powerful Mamluk Sultanate but remained a potent threat hanging over the Islamic cities of the Syrian frontier. The satisfaction in Abu'l-Feda's account of the Mamluks' conquest of the Hospitaller castle of Marqab in 1285 is clear: 'In this memorable day were revenged the evils caused by the house of the Hospitallers and the brightness of day replaced the shadows.'

The Mamluks remained the Hospitallers' primary foes during the first half of the 14th century, but thereafter the Order's relations with the sultanate in Egypt and Syria improved and, despite occasional lapses, became quite good from the later 14th to early 16th centuries. In 1403 an official treaty strengthened this relationship further and enabled the Hospitallers to assume the role of 'Protectors of the Christian Holy Places' in Palestine. The Order was even permitted to keep a consul in the Egyptian port of Damietta who could ransom captives, buy duty-free food and enjoy various other privileges. Both sides similarly agreed to give the other three months' notice of any warlike activity. Such an amicable arrangement was, unfortunately, constantly disturbed by the actions of Christian pirates, some of whom operated from Hospitaller-ruled islands in the Aegean.

In contrast the Hospitallers' relations with the closer Anatolian Turkish beyliks remained fundamentally hostile. The most threatening of these was that of the Ottomans whose forces conquered a substantial part of the Balkans to the north and west of the Aegean Sea during the second half of the 14th century. In 1392 the Hospitallers in Europe sent reinforcements, including brother-knights, to Rhodes, while at the same time trying to negotiate a truce with the Ottoman Sultan Bayazit I. The latter wanted freedom of navigation for Ottoman merchants but the Hospitallers refused. The negotiations failed and the Hospitallers anticipated an attack upon their vulnerable outpost at Smyrna (Izmir) on the Anatolian coast. Meanwhile the Hospitaller Grand Master Juan Fernandez de Heredia urged the Christian powers to launch a new crusade against the advancing Ottomans, which, when it did take place in 1396, came to grief at the battle of Nicopolis.

In 1409 the Hospitallers of Rhodes made peace with the Sultan, but relations between the Order and the fast expanding Ottoman Empire continued to be complicated by the Hospitallers' insistence that their only earthly sovereign was the Pope. While other Latin rulers in the Aegean area recognized reality and hurried to congratulate Sultan Mehmet II upon his conquest of Constantinople in 1453, the Hospitallers alone refused. Instead they tried dabbling in Ottoman politics, giving refuge to one of Mehmet II's sons, Prince Cem, during the civil war which followed the Sultan's death in 1481. Cem remained in the Order's hands as a pensioned exile and was eventually taken to France where he lived in a Hospitaller house. From then on relations between the Hospitallers and their immediate Muslim neighbours, the Ottomans, went from bad to worse while the Sultans and their advisors finally decided that this warlike Christian enclave had to go.

The Hospitaller convent church of Our Lady of Phileremos is located close to the north-western coast of the island of Rhodes, near the ancient Greek city of Ialysos. It was excessively restored in 1931 during the period of Italian rule. (David Nicolle)

A map of the city of Rhodes in a 15th-century Italian manuscript. Though stylized and unrealistic to modern eyes, this representation of the fortified city includes most of the main features, many of which can still be identified today. (British Library, London, England)

The Mongols were initially seen as a menace by the Crusader States in the mid-13th-century Middle East. The idea that the crusaders somehow missed the opportunity of forming a world-wide anti-Islamic alliance with these fearsome invaders only came later. For their part the Mongols were initially concerned about the possibility of co-operation, if not actual alliance, between the Muslims and the crusaders. The overthrow of the Ayyubids in Egypt by their own Mamluk army and the subsequent collapse of Ayyubid rule in Syria when the Mongols burst upon the scene posed serious questions for the Crusader

States and the Military Orders. Should they try to take advantage of the situation or should they wait to see what happened?

Many of the Muslims who fled from Damascus when the Mongols overran that city sought refuge in neighbouring crusader territory, or at least regarded surrendering to the Christians as preferable to being slaughtered by the Mongols. News of the Mamluk victory over a Mongol army at the battle of Ayn Jalut in Palestine in 1260 was generally welcomed in crusader territory. In fact, interest in a possible alliance with the emerging Mongol 'World Empire' appeared in Europe, including the papal court in Rome, but was less favoured in the crusader East. A few tentative, temporary and localized alliances were forged, some involving the Hospitallers through their close links with the pro-Mongol Christian Armenian Kingdom of Cilicia, but the conversion to Islam in the late

The Hospitallers acquired extensive properties in Spain as more and more territory was conquered from the Muslim Moors. For example, the Order had important estates near Lora del Rio, a small fortified town on the Guadalquivir river between Cordoba and Seville. (David Nicolle)

The Order of Hospitallers was particularly powerful and possessed substantial estates in the kingdom of Aragon, in what is now the mountainous west of Spain. This region continued to have a substantial Muslim population for centuries after the Christian conquest. Even today some of its medieval church towers, like this example at Terrer, had either served as minarets or were designed in exactly the same manner as minarets. (David Nicolle)

13th and early 14th centuries of the western Mongol *khanates* or states which emerged from the fragmentation of Genghis Khan's world empire shattered the dreams that some held of a grand alliance against Islam.

RIVALRY AMONGST THE MILITARY ORDERS

Serious rivalry between the Military Orders did not really emerge until the later 12th century, though tensions had occasionally flared up earlier. In February 1179, for example, an agreement between the Masters of the Hospital and of the Temple referred to the 'plundering of the bedouin of the Temple by the Turcopoles of Jibelin' (the Hospitaller castle at Bayt Jibrin). This agreement sought to avoid further misunderstandings in future. The admittedly unclear evidence from the campaign that culminated in Saladin's great victory at the battle of Hattin seems to suggest that, in military terms, the Hospitallers were junior partners compared to the Templars. Rivalry became more of a problem early in the 13th century, as when the Hospitallers and King Hugh I of Cyprus supported Leo of Armenia and Raymond Rupen against Bohemond IV who was supported by the Templars for succession to the Principality of Antioch. It was from then on that strong political links developed between the Lusignan ruling house of Cyprus and the Military Order of Hospitallers.

Gaspare da Vimercate in a wall-painting of St John the Baptist by Marco d'Oggiono. This Hospitaller brother fought alongside the famous Italian condottiere or mercenary leader, Francesco Sforza, in 1450. (in situ, Church of Santa Maria delle Grazie, Milan, Italy; 2006/Alinari/TopFoto)

Beneath this 15th-century carving of St George are three heraldic shields, those on the left and right almost certainly identifying the nobleman who donated money for the construction of this part of the fortifications of Bodrum. The coat-of-arms on the central shield is quartered with the Cross of the Order of the Hospitallers and may represent the arms of the Grand Masters Antonio de Fluvia (1421–37) or Jean de Lastic (1437–54). (in situ, Bodrum castle; Mary Orr)

Even more dramatic were those occasions when the Hospitallers and Templars made rival alliances with neighbouring Muslim rulers when the latter were divided by civil wars. The most notable example of this was probably during the crusade of 1239–41, which had to decide which of the competing Muslim rulers to attack. The Templars wanted to support the Ayyubid ruler of Damascus whereas the Hospitallers wanted to support the Ayyubid ruler of Cairo. In the event the Templars won the argument and a peace agreement was signed with Damascus, resulting in the Kingdom of Jerusalem gaining control of considerable territory without fighting. Most of this land was soon lost again and it is also

The great Hospitaller castle of Crac des Chevaliers in the early morning. During spring mist often forms in the fertile valley beneath the castle. This area of Syria is, in fact, very fertile and most of the nearby villages are largely Christian. (David Nicolle)

unclear how much the crusader kingdom was actually able to control because local Muslim governors often resisted, even when their ruler ordered them to hand their land over to the Christians.

Quarrels and occasional minor conflicts between Hospitallers and Templars were seen as very shocking in Europe and contributed to a growing opinion that these Military Orders were not only greedy for wealth but could be blamed for crusader defeats, largely because of their perceived lack of unity in the face of the enemy. Meanwhile some other Christian scholars were suggesting that the Military Orders' aggressiveness made the conversion of 'heathen' non-Christians more difficult.

With criticism thus seemingly being aimed at the Orders from all sides, the idea of combining the Hospitallers, Templars and even Teutonic Knights into a single Christian Military Order was raised on several occasions, especially after the fall of Acre. One such suggestion was made by the Provincial Council of Canterbury in February 1292. It proposed a new crusade to be accompanied by the unification of the Templars and Hospitallers. 'To prevent the damages and dangers which are said to have too frequently arisen from some people's division and dissent, it seems very much expedient that the Templars and Hospitallers and all the other orders of knighthood who are bound by their profession to guard the Patrimony of the Crucified One with armed force, should be combined into one order or union of religious observance as quickly as possible'. As with all the other such proposals, it came to nothing.

Another idea was to remove this shocking rivalry by allocating the Military Orders different and geographically separate 'fronts', or at least to consolidate their properties near such frontier zones. In a way this problem was dramatically solved by the trial, condemnation and subsequent dissolution of the Templars early in the 14th century. Even then, however, the Hospitallers continued to have a high opinion of their much criticized and now defunct rivals. Having inherited so much ex-Templar property, the new Hospitaller owners seemingly felt themselves honoured to follow in the footsteps of what they continued to describe as 'so noble a body'.

The Hospitallers were involved in suppressing banditry along the pilgrimage road to Santiago in north-western Spain from an early date and, like the Templars, soon had a strong presence in the kingdom of Aragon in north-eastern Spain. Throughout the Iberian peninsula the Order nevertheless faced competition from local Spanish Military Orders for recruits, donations and royal patronage.

Relations between the Hospitallers and the Order of Teutonic Knights were initially close, with the younger German Order emerging under the wing of the longer-established Hospitallers. However, as the Teutonic Knights began to exert their independence a number of quarrels flared up. One concerned the burial of deceased brethren. Because the Hospitallers wanted to control all hospitals within the Crusader States, they banned the interment of high-ranking persons within the 'House of the Germans'; namely the Teutonic Knights' hospital. The ban may also have been in an effort to ensure that deathbed donations went to the Hospitallers. The Hospitallers even threatened to remove the bodies by force to their own house. As a result the Teutonic Knights sought protection from the Templars. Once the Germans were recognized as an independent Military Order such tensions largely disappeared.

St George slaying the infidels, illustrating the divine support that the First Crusade was believed to have received outside the walls of Antioch. This early 12th-century Anglo-Norman interpretation of the event also shows crusaders praying on the left side of the carved lintel. (in situ, church of St George, Fordington, England; David Nicolle)

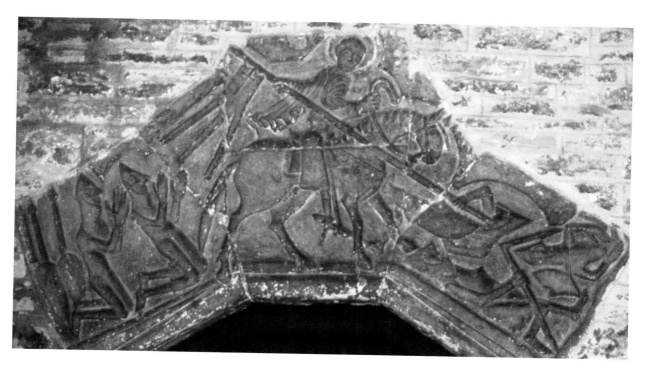

SUPPORT FOR THE HOSPITALLERS

While it was clearly important for the Order of Hospitallers to maintain good relations with the papacy, and reasonable ones with the secular rulers of the Latin Catholic states, it was equally vital for the Order to win and maintain support from ordinary people, who were its primary source of gifts of money and land. This was especially true of the knightly class from which the Hospitallers drew most of their recruits. In many respects, however, the Hospitallers took advantage of the financial and military problems faced by the castle-holding aristocracies of the Crusader States, using their own increasing financial strength to buy out such lords or taking over territory in dangerous frontier zones in return for sometimes quite limited amounts of money. Like the other Military Orders, the Hospitallers also purchased decaying or defunct religious foundations in the Holy Land and elsewhere. One such example was their purchase of the monastery on Mount Tabor in northern Palestine, which had recently been destroyed by Mamluk raiders in 1263. Here the Hospitallers absorbed the few surviving monks into their own Order, along with the extensive and fertile lands dependent upon the old monastery.

A similar process was seen in Western Europe. In Spain, for example, the first recorded donation to the Hospitallers was in Catalonia in 1108, much earlier than any known donation to the Templars. Despite a widespread opinion amongst the clergy that the Military Orders were inferior to ordinary monks because their vocation included the spilling of blood, and the fact that their military duties prevented them from keeping all the required religious vigils, the wider lay community often saw these Military Orders as the best part of the Church. This was clear throughout much of the 13th century, though by the late century the reputation of even these 'warrior monks' was declining.

In most parts of Western and Central Europe, land tended to be donated to the Hospitallers by the lower and middle nobility rather than by the upper aristocracy. Yet there were plenty of exceptions. In England, for example, Earl William I of Derby resumed his family's crusading activities by taking part in the Third Crusade. William's involvement was also reflected in a grant of lands by him and his wife to the Hospitaller Preceptory of Dingley in Northamptonshire. However, the late 12th and 13th centuries saw a sometimes quite marked decline in enthusiasm for the crusades throughout most of Europe, and this not only reduced the flow of recruits but also of donations of land and other assets. As a result the bulk of the Hospitallers' land acquisitions took place before the mid-13th century, and were followed by a decline in other religious donations.

Of course some aristocratic families continued their own tradition of support for particular Military Orders. Sometimes this was as an alternative to going on crusade themselves, but it was also a result of individuals who were impressed by

The Orthodox Monastery of St George stands in a valley overlooked by the ex-Hospitaller castle of Crac des Chevaliers. When the castle and surrounding area fell to the Mamluks in 1271, Sultan Baybars handed the monastery back to the local Orthodox Christians. It has remained, and indeed flourished, as a centre of Orthodox worship, pilgrimage and hospitality ever since. The buildings have been considerably extended in recent years. (David Nicolle)

what they had seen on crusade or during a pilgrimage. There were still some donations during the 14th, 15th and even early 16th centuries. A few of these came from local rulers and were the result of religious enthusiasm, though often they were in return for the Hospitallers promising to offer chantry masses for the donor's soul. In 1302, for example, Duke Henry II of Mecklenburg made such a conditional gift, 'so that they may remember in their prayers all of us who have been mentioned, and so that we may be regarded by God as participants in the prayers, fasts, masses, almsgiving, punishments and all holy works which the brothers of the aforesaid Order perform or carry out throughout the world for all time'.

It was soon quite normal for the Hospitallers' dwindling number of aristocratic patrons only to donate to the Order in return for specific duties such as the maintenance of chantry priests who would pray for the souls of the donor for ever. Still, some aristocratic families formed what almost amounted to alliances with one of the Military Orders, either for political reasons within their own regions or in the hope of divine reward. At the same time, the tiny clique of senior men at the very top of the Orders' hierarchy was increasingly drawn from a small number of noble families whose rivalries were echoed by their members jockeying for position and financial reward within the Military Orders. Sometimes this went so far that senior men used their own positions within the Orders to advance the interests of their families outside.

At the other end of the social scale, however, the Military Orders were now often seen by the peasantry as preferable to their previous secular lords and there were occasions, for example in the flourishing English county of Essex, where prosperous peasants bought out their existing cash-strapped feudal lords on condition that these lords donated land to the Hospitallers.

Organization and Command Structure

The Hospitallers' first convent had been in Jerusalem, but following Saladin's liberation of the Holy City in 1187 and the Third Crusade's subsequent recapture of the Palestinian coast, this convent was moved to Acre. However, the Order's main military effort was concentrated around the mighty castles of Crac des Chevaliers and Marqab. Some men managed to spend almost their entire careers on active service here, but there also seems to have been some form of rotation. Individual members of the Order would go on caravan, a word which could mean a tour of duty in the Holy Land or a raid launched against neighbouring Islamic territory.

Yet only a small proportion of the Hospitallers' personnel was ever stationed in the Middle East at any one time. Many more, including a reserve of available knights, remained in Europe to be sent East when required, or when Hospitaller finances permitted. This strategic reserve was so widely spread that most Hospitaller convents in the Christian heartlands of Western Europe, as well as in Central and Eastern Europe, contained at most a handful of properly equipped fighting men. Most Hospitallers in the West were non-military sergeants, or non-noble soldiers, who did, however, control increasingly large estates and what most people at the time believed to be huge wealth.

During the 12th and 13th centuries the differing ranks within the Order of Hospitallers were of status rather than of kind. Brother-knights and brother-sergeants had essentially the same military equipment, though that of the sergeants tended to be lighter or more limited. Both served primarily as cavalry, though at first only the knights had squires to assist them, and both were also allocated a larger number of horses. The lighter armour issued to sergeants may similarly have made them better suited to fighting on foot when the need arose. In the earliest days there was little division between the brothers-at-arms

OPPOSITE

Brothers at mass during an earthquake that severely damaged the fortifications of Rhodes in 1481. The earthquake is represented by the shattered buildings and panic-stricken people in the upper left corner. It is also worth noting that the Hospitaller brethren are joined in prayer by Western European civilians, men, women and a child. (Obsidionis Rhodie Urbis Descriptio by William Caoursin, f.120v, MS. Lat. 6067, Bibliothèque Nationale de France, Paris)

and the non-military brothers-at-service, but by the 13th century four main groups had emerged. These were the knights or brother-knights-in-arms; the brother-sergeants-at-arms; the non-military brothers-in-office; and the smaller number of chaplains or priests. The most important division was that between ordained priests and ordinary brethren, though the latter were monks. However, social divisions between the brother-knights and brother-sergeants hardened during the 13th century, reflecting a similar hardening of class divisions in the world outside. Increasing concern for lineage also meant that those of illegitimate birth were only allowed a limited amount of authority by the late 13th century. In 1262 it was decreed that only a brother-knight could become Master of the Order and by 1320 brother-knights even took precedence over priests, unless the latter were of noble birth.

The Hospitallers' system of internal government and administration reflected that of Western European secular governments. The most important official remained the Master, who was elected by committee, served for the remainder of his life, and was allowed his own household and servants. The Grand Commander was the Master's administrative second-in-command and took charge of the central convent in Palestine when the Master was absent. Normally

Wall-painting of a young Hospitaller brother by Pinturicchio, perhaps representing Alberto Aringhierre. He has the finest early 16th-century armour beneath his red and white tabard, while on the ground in front of him is an open-faced salet helmet and a pair of gauntlets. (in situ, chapel of John the Baptist, cathedral, Siena, Italy; 2006 Alinari/TopFoto)

The effigy of Roberto Sanseverino portrays this famous condottiere in the finest northern Italian 'white harness' or full-plated cuirass and limb defences of the late 15th century. Only the wealthiest or most prestigious men, including senior Hospitallers, would have had such superb armour. (in situ, cathedral, Trento, Italy; David Nicolle)

he was responsible for supplies, domestic administration and the Order's properties in the Middle East. Some part of the weapons store was also under the Grand Commander's control and by 1303 the Arbalestry or vitally important crossbow-store was one of his bailliwicks or areas of responsibility.

In all other respects it was the Marshal who was the leading military official within the Order. His position was first mentioned in the 1160s but the increasing militarization of the Hospitallers inevitably resulted in an increase in the Marshal's initially rather limited responsibilities and thus his status. At first the Marshal only held the strategically important Commandery (the Order's smallest territorial division) of Tiberius, but following a widespread military restructuring of the Order in 1206 his powers were placed upon a new statutory basis while all brethren-in-arms, both knights and sergeants, were now under his authority. As a result the Marshal became responsible for discipline in the central convent where he was regarded as leader of the fighting men, whereas the Grand Commander was seen as the Master's representative.

The Marshal's office continued to distribute military equipment and horses and was in charge of the forge and of saddlery, as well as issuing rations and clothing to those sent on missions away from the convent. On campaign the Marshal now commanded Hospitaller forces under the immediate authority of the Master or his Lieutenant, and led the field army if the Master was absent. All military officers in the Middle East were under the Marshal to some extent, though this varied

The ruins of the Latin cathedral of Our Lady of the Bourg in the old city of Rhodes. It is now bisected by a road leading down to the inner harbour. After Rhodes fell to the Ottoman Turks all 'Latins' or Catholic Christians were expelled from the fortified city, though Orthodox Greek Christians remained. (David Nicolle)

The small Orthodox church of Santa Nikola, near the Gate of St Athanasiou in the walled city of Rhodes, dates from the 15th century. Here in the southernmost part of the Hospitaller-ruled city, the local Greeks were allowed to practise their religion almost unhindered, and continued to do so under Turkish rule. (David Nicolle)

in day-to-day practice. The only exceptions were capitular baillis (senior officers in charge of various bailliwicks) and the immediate companions of the Master himself. Lesser military officers such as the Master Esquire, Gonfalonier and Commander of Knights were again under the Marshal, as were almost all castellans or castle commanders after 1303, along with the Turcopolier in time of war and the Admiral if the Marshal was present with the fleet.

As the second most senior conventual bailli (official at the Central Convent) after the Grand Commander, the Marshal reported on his responsibilities directly to the Chapter General or 'governing committee' of the Order. His insignia of office consisted of the Order's banner, a purse and a seal. The Marshal's standard-bearer was the Gonfalonier or standard-bearer of the Order as a whole. Since 1206 he had been allowed four horses, two squires and two pack-animals to carry his equipment, plus one driver. A further regulation of 1268 specified that the Marshal was allowed a *turcoman*, hack or riding horse, in addition to his *destrier* or warhorse, though this had to be made available for use by a brother-in-arms if needed in battle. In 1302 the Marshal's allocation of horses was increased to five, with three grooms in addition to his squire, chamberlain, page, butler, sergeant and cook.

As the senior military figure in the Order, the Marshal was widely consulted for his expertise on Middle Eastern affairs, both political and military. However, his power tended to be reduced by the simple fact that those holding the office of Marshal were changed so often, almost annually in the early 14th century. Military equipment donated to the Order by outsiders in the 13th century went to the Marshal's office unless it had been specifically given to the castles of Crac des Chevaliers or Marqab, before these fortresses fell to the Mamluks.

Nevertheless, there were still tensions between the Marshal and the Treasury, since the latter had to pay for anything else that the Marshal's office issued. Furthermore, the Marshal could requisition any such items from local commanders. The Marshal's office or Marshalsy consisted of two main departments. Perhaps the most important was the weapons store, where at least one brother-in-arms had to be responsible for looking after all military equipment except crossbows, which were kept in the Arbalestry under the Grand Commander's authority. The second department of the Marshalsy was the stables, which had to deal with a perpetual shortage of horses, the problems of maintaining the health of mounts and a chronic wastage of animals brought by sea from Europe.

The Constable was another senior military officer, though his responsibilities focussed on organizational matters. This role was first mentioned in 1126 and its holder remained a subordinate or deputy of the Marshal for more than 40 years. The role of Master Esquire of the main or central convent seems to date from a major military reorganization in 1206. He was thereafter in charge of squires and grooms, supervising all work concerning horses and stables. As such the Master Esquire was the immediate superior of the Crie, Acrie or Cria who was in immediate charge of the stables themselves. The stables was an organization rather than a building or series of buildings, and it issued mounts as well as perhaps harness to brethren-in-arms. As such it may have served as a kind of remount depot. The Master Esquire certainly reclaimed the horses of deceased brethren on behalf of the Marshal and while on campaigns or raids he was responsible for the discipline and welfare of squires as well as horses. In practice, therefore, the Master Esquire was normally one of the most senior and experienced brother-sergeants, being issued with three horses and having his own household including squires. He should not be confused with another Master Esquire who led the Master's own squires and was later called the Grand Esquire.

The Gonfalonier or Standard-Bearer of the Order of Hospitallers was placed beneath the Marshal following the reorganization of 1206. He was in charge of the Banner of the Order and from 1270 onwards had to be a brother-knight of legitimate birth. This position seems to have been offered as a reward for notable skill or courage in battle. Certainly a Gonfalonier had to be a steady and reliable man since brethren-in-arms were bound to follow his banner in combat. The Gonfalonier could himself lead raids if the Master, his Lieutenant or the Marshal were not available, though these were only likely to have been small-scale operations. Nevertheless the Gonfalonier's authority and freedom of action did increase as the years passed.

The title of Commander of Knights was first recorded in 1220, being appointed to lead the knights if the Marshal or his Lieutenant were not available. This remained, however, a relatively junior position. Other subordinate officials included the Commander of the Vault who was in charge of stores under the authority of the Grand Commander, the Sub-Marshal and the Turcopolier. The latter commanded the turcopoles and was first mentioned in a Hospitaller context in 1203. By 1248 he was a brother-in-arms, though probably only a brother-sergeant. In 1303 the office of Turcopolier was raised to the rank of a Conventual Bailliwick, though its holder was still under the Marshal in military matters, administration and the deployment of his troops. To cover his costs the Turcopolier was eventually assigned 100 Saracen bezants or gold coins per year, with 50 measures, or large barrels, of wine from two designated vineyards in Cyprus.

The castellans, or commanders of the Order's most important castles, were under the Marshal's authority, though in time of peace the Marshal seems to have shared this with the main chapter or governing committee of the Order. Some of the smaller castles do not seem to have had castellans and some may not even have had permanent garrisons. In 1206 every castellan in Syria was allocated three horses, two squires and a turcopole. The castellans of the main castles of Syria and Palestine, such as Belvoir, Belmont, Bayt Jibrin, Crac des Chevaliers, Marqab, Mount Tabor, as well as Selifke in Cilicia and perhaps a few others, achieved the status of capitular baillis. Furthermore, in 1304, after all the Syrian castles had fallen to Mamluk reconquest, no brother could become a castellan unless he had served in the Order for at least five years.

RIGHT

*St John the Baptist in his
identifying cloak of animal skin
is here shown also wearing the
cloak of a Hospitaller brother.
The panel-painting forms part of
a triptych by Giovanni del
Biondo, an Italian painter of the
Gothic school who is known to
have worked in Florence between
1356 and 1399. (Italy,
Florence, Accademia; 2006
Alinari/TopFoto)*

OPPOSITE

*Burning the bones of St John, in
a late 15th-century painting by
an artist known as Geertgen van
tot St Jijn who may himself have
been a Hospitaller brother. Those
dressed in Hospitaller costume,
who are observing the scene in
this picture, clearly represent
specific individuals from the time
of the painting, though their
names have since been lost.
(akg-images/Erich Lessing)*

The role of Admiral of the Order of the Hospitallers was one of the last military titles to be created, and dated from around 1300. He was in command of all galleys and armed ships smaller than a galley, as well as of all troops and sailors aboard such vessels. Crews, including the marines, were not themselves brethren of the Order but were mercenaries paid by the Hospitallers' Treasury.

A huge, widely spread and wealthy organization like that of the Hospitallers naturally needed a large number of skilled civilian or non-military officials. These included the Drapier, first mentioned in 1206, who was in charge of clothing allocations from the Parmentarie or clothing store. He wore a purse as a mark of rank and was also given a seal at some time during the 13th century. The Parmentarie seems to have been a tailoring department as well as clothing store and here the Drapier was assisted by a brother-of-the-parmentarie. The latter

had various duties including sealing up the goods of deceased brothers. The Drapier would take their robes, any cloth, bed-linen and hats, perhaps for reuse, although the Drapier was also recorded as distributing the effects of the dead to the neighbouring poor. The Treasurer in charge of the Treasury was another such non-military brother official, as was the Hospitaller responsible for the sick and the Conventual Prior who was the Order's most senior ecclesiastical official.

Further specialized officials were not themselves brethren of the Order. Those with military responsibilities included the Master Crossbowman and Master Sergeant who were not permitted to eat at the same table at the brethren. Both were probably laymen hired to take charge of mercenary soldiers in the Order's service.

The reality of Hospitaller military and economic power was recognized by the Church hierarchy in both Jerusalem and Rome during the 12th century and in 1154 a papal bull permitted them to have their own priests. Such priests were normally under the same discipline as the brother-knights, though in more important matters those in the Middle East were subject to the Conventual Prior while those in Europe were subject to their regional priors. As a result the Order of the Hospitallers was largely independent of the rest of the local Church hierarchy. After the Latin or Catholic episcopal see (bishop's base or headquarters) at Banyas on the Syrian coast was destroyed by Saladin's victorious army, the Bishop moved to the Hospitaller castle of Marqab, adding considerably to the Order's prestige. Meanwhile the Pope naturally retained overall jurisdiction but only seems to have been asked to pass a judgement when the Rules of the Order were being changed.

FIGHTING BRETHREN AND OTHER FIGHTING MEN

Hospitaller records are detailed and abundant enough to make the question of numbers of men – brethren and non-brethren – slightly clearer than is normally the case with medieval armies. Around 1169, for example, the Hospitaller Grand Master Gilbert d'Assailly promised to supply 500 knights and 500 turcopoles for a forthcoming invasion of Egypt. Not all of them would have been brethren of the Order. Nor were the estimated 2,000 men whom the Hospitallers were said to have had at the siege of Damietta during the Fifth Crusade. The Military Orders were not obliged to maintain a specified number of troops in return for the lands that had been given to them.

In fact, the evidence indicates that the Hospitallers normally only had around 300 brethren-at-arms in the Middle East, though at times this figure was greater, plus non-brethren sergeants, turcopoles, support personnel and so on. So the substantial force of 100 knights, 400 mounted sergeants and 500 infantry

A woodcut print showing brethren giving alms to the poor in a version of the Statutes of the Order by the Chancellor, published in Ulm in 1493. (Library of the Order of St John, St John's Gate, London)

sergeants that the Hospitallers raised to attack Hama in 1232–33 clearly could not all have been brethren. Ten years later the Hospitallers suffered catastrophic casualties at the battle of La Forbie. Here 325 brethren-in-arms and around 200 turcopoles were lost, only 26 Hospitallers escaping, which must have virtually wiped out the brethren-at-arms currently stationed in the Middle East. Just over 20 years later a letter by the Hospitaller Grand Master Hugh Revel implied that there were once again only some 300 brothers in Syria, compared

'The Crucifixion' forms one of the finest manuscript illustrations in The Rhodes Missal, *which dates from the early 15th century. It was made in France and was then sent, along with other gifts, to the Hospitaller mother house in Rhodes. (Library of the Order of St John, St John's Gate, London)*

to the 10,000 'once fed by the Order'. The latter figure was clearly a considerable exaggeration, though it might have indicated the larger number of mercenaries once maintained by the Order in the Middle East. By 1301, following the fall of Acre, the number of Hospitallers based at Limassol in Cyprus had slumped to a mere 70 brother-knights and ten brother-sergeants.

Although there were larger numbers of Hospitaller brethren elsewhere, they tended to be spread over a wide area. In the other frontier regions such as Iberia their numbers were even smaller than in the Middle East, 30 brother-knights being requested to help defend the frontier of Valencia in the late 13th century and 60 being demanded to fend off a feared attack from Granada in the early 14th century. Even these small figures were probably not actually achieved. Hungary was another frontier zone in the mid-13th century and here the Hospitallers agreed to supply 100 brethren-in-arms in return for authority in the area of Severin (now in south-western Romania), which they also agreed to defend. But, in the event, only 60 such brothers seem to have been there when the Mongols invaded.

The number of Hospitaller brethren stationed in any particular place did not represent the entire military strength of the garrison in question. In practice the numbers of mercenaries and other personnel were normally far greater. In 1203 the garrisons of the great castles of Crac des Chevaliers and Marqab combined to attack Ba'tin with 400 cavalry and 1,100 infantry, plus an unspecified number of turcopoles. Nine years later these same castles housed 2,000 and 1,000 troops respectively, but in a letter to the Pope dated 1255 the Hospitallers claimed that they only planned to have 60 cavalry in Crac and 40 in the rebuilt fortification on Mount Tabor, so perhaps they were only referring to brethren-in-arms. When the Hospitaller-held town of Arsuf fell to the Mamluks in 1265, 1,000 men were killed or captured, but only 80 of them were Hospitaller brethren. Fifteen years later the garrison of Marqab included 600 cavalry alone, but in 1282 the Master sent only 50 brother-knights and 50 turcopoles to help defend Armenian Cilicia. Wherever they were stationed, the Hospitaller brothers-in-arms clearly formed an elite, however small their number.

ECONOMIC SUPPORT FOR THE ORDER

In addition to defending what remained of the Crusader States, the Hospitallers used their Middle Eastern estates and other economic assets to support their defence by growing food and raising money through the export of olive oil and cane sugar. Most of the Hospitaller estates in Palestine, Lebanon and Syria were owned freehold, while the local Christian and Muslim peasantry were attached to their Hospitaller lords according to earlier Byzantine, Armenian or Islamic

An engraved portrait of an unnamed Grand Master of the Hospitallers, made by Martino Rota in 1565. It is thought to have been based upon a portrait of Jean Parisot de la Valette by Titian. No other contemporary portraits are known to exist. (Museum of the Order of St John, London)

laws. Western European-style serfdom was extremely rare and most of the Hospitallers' peasants remained free men. The local Hospitaller castellan or bailli normally dealt with them through their own headman. Such headmen were often in charge of two or three *casalia* or villages, where he and his assistants were responsible for maintaining law and order and the suppression of local banditry

A relatively small and isolated coastal tower right next to the coast and within sight of the massive Hospitaller castle of Marqab may have served as a defensible customs post. Its garrison would not have been large enough to stop a determined enemy force passing along the coastal road from which this photograph was taken. (David Nicolle)

as well as supervising the work of the peasants themselves. The taxes from such villages were initially a dependable and valuable source of income, but as the Crusader States contracted, so the villages began to refuse to pay.

The territory held by the Hospitallers in the Crusader States was not particularly extensive but tended to be compact and fertile. This was clearly the case with the Order's palatinate centred on Crac des Chevaliers.

Like other major landowners in the Crusader States, the Hospitallers owned many Muslim slaves. Some they had captured themselves, some were given by their vassals as the Hospitallers' share of booty after a successful campaign, while other slaves were purchased on the open market. These latter unfortunates were not used for prisoner exchange but as agricultural, domestic or urban labour. Some may have been amongst those ransomed by a Muslim merchant from Damascus in 1266; those released were described as 'prisoners held by the Hospitallers on Crac des Chevaliers'. Other slaves purchased their own freedom, but only at a price that enabled the Hospitallers to buy two or three replacements. In time of crisis the release of large numbers of prisoners, both men and women, could buy off a threatened Islamic attack. The fate of the numerous male and female Muslim slaves who were shipped back to Europe in the 13th century remains unknown, but there were many such people in Italy a century later.

Communications between the Middle East and Western Europe by sea were the life-blood of the Crusader States once the overland route was effectively severed in the mid-12th century. After 1187 the Crusader States were substantially dependent upon imported food from Sicily, southern Italy and southern France, as well as being forced to import military equipment and horses. As the situation worsened in the 13th century, live meat was even being shipped to the Crusader States. Such a system of long-distance supply necessitated very

The so-called 'Crypt of St John' was in fact the refectory of the Hospitaller headquarters or mother house in Acre. It is believed to date from the mid-13th century when King Louis IX of France arrived on crusade and offered to pay for its construction. (David Nicolle)

sophisticated administrative and financial structures. The Italians played the major role, but the Military Orders including the Hospitallers also took part. Marseilles was the assembly point for men and matériel to be sent from the Western European priories to the Holy Land.

With their wide-ranging network of subordinate houses, dedicated and generally literate personnel plus their already considerable wealth, the Hospitallers were better able to send men and money from otherwise neglected regions than were most secular authorities. For example, Central and Eastern Europe were apparently linked to the Middle East via the river Danube, the Balkans and the Byzantine capital of Constantinople. In 1181 or 1182 there was a Hospitaller prior based in Constantinople who forwarded 200 rolls of cloth to his superiors in Jerusalem; this is unlikely to have been an isolated case. The Byzantine capital may have been the main collection point for financial revenues from the Hospitaller houses in East and Central Europe. Certainly there was a Hospitaller *domus* or house and a church in Constantinople itself. When this route became too dangerous as a result of declining Byzantine control in the Balkans, it was replaced by overland routes to Venice and thence by sea to Syria.

The Great Hall or chapter house in the Hospitaller castle of Crac des Chevaliers is a classic example of Gothic architecture and dates from the early to mid-13th century. To the left were the kitchens, while to the right was a small but highly decorated cloister leading to the central courtyard of the castle. (David Nicolle)

The Military Orders were not alone in being wealthy by the standards of their day, and it was the thriving commercial prosperity of the remaining Crusader States that enabled them to import goods in such volumes. However, the secular rulers of the Crusader States and the Military Orders both faced huge expenditures. For the Hospitallers this primarily concerned the provision of horses, where wastage due to warfare and disease remained very high, and the maintenance of expensive, heavily armoured troops including numerous mercenaries. Consequently the Hospitallers, like the other Military Orders, were finding themselves seriously short of money by the late 13th century, a situation which had become acute by the early 14th century.

Unfortunately this financial reality appeared almost unbelievable to ordinary people, who saw only the Order's wealth in terms of land, revenues and other sources of income. For its part, the Hospitaller headquarters in the Middle East often complained that it was not receiving sufficient support from the Western priories, particularly in terms of cash. Within Western Europe the subordinate Hospitaller establishments normally sent about one-third of their revenues to their local priory, and this proportion later became a fixed sum. If required, they might have to hand over all their surplus revenues. Other sources of income were welcome but less predictable and included booty from frontier regions when warfare favoured the crusaders. By the early 14th century the Order was also earning money from banking, though not to the same extent as the Templars.

Revenues from the islands were largely kept separate from the revenues sent by the European priories, not that they amounted to much. Rhodes and some other islands produced sugar, honey, soap and canvas for sails. The little island of Nísíros also produced volcanic sulphur and figs, while a few islands produced salt. The only major exceptions in the eastern Mediterranean region were the Order's valuable sugar plantations in Cyprus. Although the Hospitallers' few estates in mainland Greece were an additional, if minor, source of revenue, it was the Order's extensive possessions in Western and Central Europe that continued to provide its real financial strength.

ORGANIZATION DURING THE 14TH AND 15TH CENTURIES

The Order of St John was a highly bureaucratic organization in which every priory was expected to keep detailed records of its rents, incomes and properties. Record keeping must have taken up much of many brothers' time; the entire system was supposedly directed by the Master and his household in Rhodes, although, at least in the 14th century, many Hospitaller Masters were elderly and well-meaning, but somewhat ineffective as leaders.

In Rhodes the Master also minted coins, granted land, supervised taxation, managed local justice and, when necessary, dispensed justice throughout the Order. He acted with the agreement of the Convent Council, which was, at least theoretically, his superior. For the Hospitallers, the only earthly authority that ranked superior to that of their Convent Council was the Pope himself. The Master usually resided in Rhodes, though in times of financial crisis he could be away for an extended period, on one occasion for no less than 13 years.

The Hospitaller castle of Crac des Chevaliers served as a convent for the Order of Hospitallers, as well as a fortress. That was presumably why a decorated but rudimentary covered cloister was built in the already cramped central courtyard. (David Nicolle)

The Order's possessions in Europe had been grouped into regions called priories since the 12th century, but now the system of *langues*, 'tongues' or broad linguistic groupings, also appeared in the East. It had started in Cyprus and was completed in Rhodes. Initially there were five such langues but their number was eventually increased to seven, three of which largely stemmed from the kingdom of France – one French and two Provençal. Each langue was of equal status and each was represented in the Chapter General or central council of the Order in Rhodes. Each langue was also headed by a man known as its *pilier* or 'pillar' who, from 1320 onwards, had one of the great offices of the Order reserved for him. Thus the Grand Commander now came from Provence, the Marshal from Auvergne, the Hospitaller from France, the Drapier from Spain, the Admiral (whose position steadily increased in importance as the Order refocussed on naval warfare) from Italy, and the Turcopolier from England. Nothing was specifically set aside for Germany and most of the German Langue left Rhodes around 1340. Nor was the role of Treasurer attached to a specific langue, but from the start of the 15th century the office of Drapier's Lieutenant was traditionally given to a Spaniard.

During the 15th century the pilier of each langue could also claim a priory and its revenues when one became vacant, though he often had to wait several years for this to happen. In 1330 the Master won the right to grant two commanderies in each priory every ten years to brother-knights currently serving in the central convent in Rhodes. This was presumably to provide revenues to maintain such men.

Garrisons

The primary task of brethren in the East remained military, and the defence of the city of Rhodes itself was organized by langues, each of which was allocated a length of the city wall. The number of brethren in Rhodes and the islands meanwhile increased as the Order's finances stabilized. In earlier centuries there had rarely been more than 300 brother-knights in Syria and the Holy Land but this soon rose to 400 in Rhodes.

By the time of the Ottoman siege in 1480 the garrison of Rhodes consisted of around 450 brother-knights and 150 brother-sergeants, plus from 1,500 to 2,000 other soldiers excluding local militias. However, most of the brother-knights had command or administrative roles, some being too old to fight while others were currently garrisoning distant castles or were aboard ship. Perhaps 250 were actually available to help man the walls. A partial roll-call of brother-knights and sergeants at the start of the final Ottoman siege in 1522 listed 290 brother-knights, 15 *donati* (noblemen waiting to join as full brothers), about 300 brother-sergeants-at-arms, plus around 950 European sailors and soldiers and several thousand local Rhodian militia.

The acute dog-leg turn in the covered entrance slope of the Hospitaller castle of Crac des Chevaliers. The passage to the right leads down to the main entrance while that on the left leads up to the central courtyard. There was also a small stables on the right, though the main stables was a much larger structure accessed from behind the position where this photograph was taken. (David Nicolle)

The garrisons of other Hospitaller outposts in the Aegean were much smaller. In the early 15th century the bailli or commander of Lango (Kos) usually commanded around 25 brethren, plus ten other Latins (meaning Western European men-at-arms), 100 turcopoles, a doctor, an apothecary and a galley with 20 rowing benches. Every brother-knight in Rhodes had to spend at least one year serving in the Lango garrison.

Priors and Priories
The biggest administrative and logistical problems that the Order persistently faced were great distances and the slowness or unreliability of medieval communications. It was obviously difficult adequately to supervise their scattered estates and so the Order attempted to delegate authority, especially to priors who served at the greatest distance from the Hospitallers' headquarters convent. Unfortunately the system of visitation, or regular inspections, by representatives from this central convent in Rhodes was inadequate and many priors failed to visit the convent as often as they were supposed to do. The result was widespread inefficiency if not downright corruption.

Since the primary purpose of these European estates was to support the fighting men in the Aegean as they had earlier supported the fighting men in Syria, those in charge were duty bound to maximize revenues by making the best possible use of the land or other assets available in each region. Sometimes

HOSPITALLER PRIORIES c. 1300

this involved economic development in quite a modern sense, not only in the improvement and extension of agriculture but in the establishment of local industries, as well as the colonization of frontier territories. This was not only to make these territories as productive as possible but also to draw them into the mainstream of medieval European civilization. Hospitaller colonization was most obvious in the still undeveloped Slav and Hungarian regions of Central Europe and in the similarly marginal Celtic areas of the British Isles.

Another priority for the Hospitallers was the consolidation of the Order's too often fragmented and scattered possessions. This was done by the priors and their subordinates selling, exchanging or buying properties. They then often invested surplus cash in additional land. Not surprisingly, perhaps, senior Hospitaller administrators became highly skilled businessmen and were recognized as such by European rulers. Several became royal advisors, though this could involve them in dangerous political issues and, where the vexed question of taxation was concerned, make them very unpopular with ordinary people.

One of the first such royal advisors was Father Guérin of the Hospital of St Sebastian, who joined King Philip Augustus of France's entourage when the king returned from the Third Crusade. He was described as 'King Philip's special counsellor in the royal palace by virtue of his wisdom and incomperable [sic] gift of council, with responsibility for royal and ecclesiastical affairs second only to the King'. As a reward Father Guérin was made Bishop of Senlis. Another chronicler wrote of Father Guérin that 'although he was distinguished in the palace, he concealed a Knight of Christ under the screen of his cloak in order that he might opportunely help Christians and comfort their hearts'. Less favourable observers maintained that Guérin became too worldly and that his actions were unsuitable for a man of religion.

Only a few Hospitaller priors reached such political prominence. Most concentrated on administering their own priories. Twenty-five priories and grand commanderies now formed the middle level of Hospitaller administration, with the langues above and the commanderies or preceptories below. The men in charge of these priories ranked as capitular baillis because they could theoretically be recalled by the Chapter General of the Order in Rhodes. Some commanders and castellans in the East also ranked as capitular baillis, and as such were equal in rank to a European prior. Most priories were based upon a distinct linguistic area, though this was not true of parts of the German priories, still less those of East-Central Europe and Scandinavia. The latter, confusingly for modern readers with some knowledge of Roman history, was called the Priory of Dacia, because Roman Dacia was located in what is now Romania.

Most priors were appointed from above and in the early 14th century usually held their office for around ten years. However, later in the century this term of office tended to get longer and by the 15th century most priories and bailliwicks were held for life. Although some men achieved positions of authority at quite a young age, the rules of the Order stated that a brother was not allowed the senior executive administrative authority that went with the rank of bailli until he was at least 25 years old. Furthermore, he had to have been in the Order for at least three years. Several priories included a large estate which served as a permanent base, both physical and financial, for its prior. In many other cases, however, he selected five commanderies within his priory to serve as his 'chambers' and as a result travelled around a great deal. This also enabled him to observe and to consult. Theoretically the prior or his senior officers should visit each commandery in the priory at least once every 25 years and then draw up a *caput breve*, or detailed report on its condition and value.

Preceptories

The basic territorial unit of the Order was now the preceptory or commandery, which could incorporate several smaller properties. The first of these may have appeared in the Iberian peninsula in the 13th century but in the early 14th century the system was imposed throughout the Order. Once again, the local preceptor was appointed by the Master, or at least with his direct authorization. A preceptor headed a convent, though houses of brother-clerics or priests rather than knights and sergeants were normally – and confusingly – called priories. The preceptor could be a brother-knight, brother-sergeant or brother-priest. Some were appointed for life, though most only served a short term before being transferred to another convent. As a result several of these men became highly experienced and valued administrators.

The Hospitallers became quite powerful in the Iberian peninsula, though here they were also in competition with indigenous Spanish and Portuguese Military Orders. They held the largely Moorish castle of Mertola in southern Portugal for many years. This had been a flourishing town during the previous Moorish Islamic centuries and the low, white-painted church to the left of the main castle tower is believed to be built on the foundation of an earlier mosque. (David Nicolle)

81

A preceptor who successfully improved the value of the land under his authority, known as his *benefice*, was then entitled to promotion to a more valuable benefice. As a result they were divided into those who were in their first appointment or *chevissement* and those who had been moved up to a *méliorissement*. The system worked remarkably well and resulted in a general improvement in the productivity of most Hospitaller estates. Exceptions tended to be found where one brother-knight held two or three commanderies at the same time, often as a result of family or political influence, or where a preceptory was held by an absentee preceptor who left his benefice to be managed by a subordinate known as a conductor.

It must be borne in mind that these same men had either served as active soldiers in Rhodes earlier in their careers or, as often happened, could find themselves summoned East to join a garrison. They were by no means soft-living bureaucrats. While serving the Order in Western or Central Europe, brethren normally lived in a Hospitaller domus under the authority of their preceptor. Most of these houses were for lay brethren, knights and sergeants rather than brother-priests. The man in charge of such a domus imposed discipline and observation of the Order's Rule, as well as administering its properties. Concubinage and sexual immorality seem to have been common amongst the brethren, though violent disorder was rarer.

Sometimes the preceptor was assisted by other officials such as another subordinate or sub-commander. A brother might also be delegated to supervise a group of outlying properties, generally living alone in one of these, which would be called a grange. His authority was strictly limited, though he would still sometimes be called a preceptor or commander. The other brethren in the domus or convent lived a limited form of communal life, administering surrounding properties through chapters or meetings that tended to be held once a week.

HOUSES IN EUROPE

Fourteenth-century Hospitaller houses could vary considerably in size, but only a minority seem to have had their own resident priest. In 1338 a detailed survey, ordered by the Pope as part of widespread reforms, shows the biggest domus in England to have been at Chippenham, which housed ten brethren, and at Clerkenwell, which was the English headquarters and housed seven brethren. While some houses in mainland Europe were considerably larger, most of those in England had only two or three brethren. The Hospitaller manor at Hether in Leicestershire may have been typical. It had been given to the Order by Ralph de Greisley in the mid-12th century. Its church and commandery may not have been built until the 1220s, but the domus at Hether soon had a refectory, hall, kitchen, vaults and dormitories. In 1279 the Prior of Hether was said to have 'one caracute of land desmesne, together with the advowson of the church, two watermills, fifteen and a half virgates of land in villeinage which ten villeins hold. Ten virgates of land is held in free tenure, held by six free tenants, and two cottages. The prior has free fishing in the waters of Shepey, but not warren.' (This in modern terms translates as 120 acres of land held for the priory's own use, together with the right to nominate the priest of the church, two watermills and 465 acres of land for serf tenants which was held by ten serf-peasants, as well as fishing rights but not the right to hunt rabbits.)

In 1351 the Hospitallers combined their local manors at Dalby, Rothley and Hether into one existing community, to be known as the Preceptory of Dalby. By that date the lands, meadow and pasture at Hether were worth an annual rent of 26s. 8d, plus a mill to clean and thicken cloth by beating and washing it; this was let for 13s. 4d while a water-mill was let for £2.10s. In 1534 the rents of the Preceptory of Hether, plus its other possessions, were assessed at £33.1s.5d, perhaps as a result of inflation as much as the Order's efforts to increase its value.

Preceptories in other parts of Europe reflected their differing local circumstances. Some in northern Italy, for example, were responsible for maintaining a stretch of road or a bridge, while those in or near the Alpine passes continued the Order's traditional hospitality towards travellers and pilgrims. Whereas Italian preceptories were rarely fortified, many in Bohemia and Moravia were surrounded by a sturdy wall or stood close to the castle of the original donor.

The number of local people who were dependent upon a Hospitaller preceptory as their landlord or feudal lord varied but could be large, up to 1,000 or even 5,000 being recorded in Aragon. The number of people living in a Hospitaller estate could also be large. For example, in 1370 the preceptor of Orta was ordered to maintain in his castle a brother-knight, a sergeant, two priests, one being a brother of the Order and the other not, plus two attendants, an altar boy, a cleaning woman, three stablemen, a baker, an oven woman, six pack-animals and two warhorses. Nor was such an arrangement likely to have been untypical.

There were also regional variations in the proportion of brother-knights to other brethren. In England in 1338 over a quarter of brethren were brother-knights, in Provence less than a quarter, while in the Priory of France only one in 20 brethren were knights. Of course, very few brethren had any real military role outside the Aegean and to some extent the Iberia peninsula. It would similarly be misleading to think that just because Hospitaller preceptories encouraged settlement and colonization, this inevitably led to violence against the indigenous inhabitants. In the British Isles, for example, the Priory of Ireland with its headquarters at Kilmainham was subject to the Priory of England. So was the one commandery in Scotland at Torphichen, well into the 14th century.

Like parts of Wales, Ireland and Scotland were regarded as frontier zones by the rulers of England. While Scottish as well as Welsh rulers were patrons of the Order, as were English kings, there is no evidence that the Hospitallers had any military role against the troublesome highland Welsh or highland Scots. Even the elements of fortification seen in some Irish preceptories probably reflected the lawless state of the country generally rather than any particular threat from or against the Celtic Irish. Nor were Hospitaller preceptories in these areas situated near the frontiers between Anglo-Norman or Anglo-Scottish and 'native' Celtic regions.

The Hospitaller prior in Ireland was sometimes involved in military action, but on these occasions he was acting just like any other liege man in defence of his king's realm or, as in 1285, as the king's Justiciar (chief minister) attempting to impose law and order. In August 1318, for example, Roger Utlagh, the prior

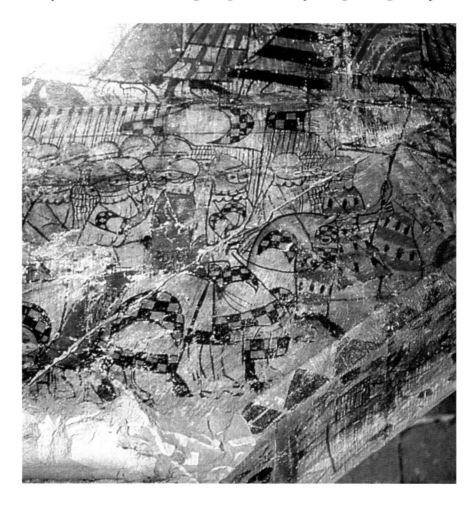

Wall-painting in the ex-Templar castle, Alcañiz, Spain. After the dissolution of the Order of Templars, their properties in this town were handed over to the Hospitallers and to the Spanish Military Order of Calatrava. The paintings are very simple and date from the late 13th or more likely 14th century, illustrating the distinctive arms and armour of the Iberian peninsula. (in situ, castle, Alcañiz, Spain)

The bridge at Puenta de la Reinha where the pilgrim roads through Navarre and Aragon joined on their way to Santiago de Compostella. The Hospitallers' possessions in this town were amongst their most valuable within the Iberian peninsula. (David Nicolle)

in Ireland, petitioned the king for compensation for the losses he had suffered during his recent service against an invasion of Ireland by a Scottish force under Edward Bruce. There were similar instances in subsequent years, but in each case the Hospitallers in Ireland were playing their part in the overall defence of an area. Meanwhile the Order generally had friendly relations with the local Celtic peoples, who were certainly not seen as enemies.

Hospitallers in the Iberian peninsula did, meanwhile, play a greater military role, though this was not always against the Muslims of al-Andalus. Those in Aragon quite often found themselves caught up in wars against the fellow-Christian kingdom of Castile, or were involved in Aragon's empire-building campaigns elsewhere in the Mediterranean. Few Aragonese brethren were summoned to do military service in Rhodes, though some were seconded for papal employment. More surprisingly, summons to serve against Islamic Granada were rare. In the mid-14th century many men living on Hospitaller estates in Aragon were offered lifetime grants of food, wine and other necessities in return for an oath to fight for the Order, though this would be at the Order's expense if the campaign fell outside the individual's immediate neighbourhood.

Normally a Grand Preceptor was in overall charge of Hospitaller priories in Germany and the rest of Central Europe, sometimes including Scandinavia, but his area of responsibility varied. A lack of strong or centralized monarchies in Germany and neighbouring Bohemia enabled the Hospitallers to continue acquiring estates and castles, which tended to draw the Order into local political rivalries. During the 14th century the Hospitaller bailliwick of Brandenburg, in

The south chapel of the crypt of the Hospitaller Priory Church in Clerkenwell, on the edge of the City of London. St John's Gate, Clerkenwell, is now the headquarters of the British Order of St John. (Order of St John, St John's Gate, London, England)

The south chapel of the crypt of the Hospitaller Priory Church in Clerkenwell, on the edge of the City of London. St John's Gate, Clerkenwell, is now the headquarters of the British Order of St John. (Order of St John, St John's Gate, London, England)

the far north-east of Germany, tried to win its independence from the German Grand Priory. The resulting struggle lasted many years, on and off, with Brandenburg taking advantage of financial crises in far away Rhodes. When in 1366 the Order sold its houses in Pomerelia to the Teutonic Knights, the rest of Brandenburg feared going the same way, which led to a rapprochement with the Grand Priory, though the matter was not finally settled until the Treaty of Heimbach in 1382. Nevertheless, the Hospitaller bailli of Brandenburg increased in power and influence until he became politically one of the most important men in the German Empire.

Meanwhile the ordinary brethren of the Order in eastern Germany and the neighbouring Slav kingdoms of Poland and Bohemia continued to be involved in a process of economic development and colonization. This originally meant converting a local Slav village to Latin Christianity, then bringing in German settler families, to the extent that some areas were effectively Germanized. Once again Hospitaller numbers remained small and apparently included both German and Slav brethren. During the first half of the 14th century, for example, there were around 30 brethren in Pomerania. This was a politically volatile region which had only been converted to Christianity in the 12th century and where the Hospitallers had three castles, two named Stargrad on the rivers Ihna and Ferse, plus Schlawe, which was also on the river Ferse.

The presence of German Hospitallers in Bohemia was not a matter of German colonization but reflected a desire on the part of local rulers and the Order itself to employ the most qualified available men in a land that was still relatively backward. As a result the Hospitaller Priory of Bohemia flourished until it was ruined during the Hussite wars of the 15th century; its prior, Heinrich von Neuhaus, was killed in battle in 1420.

Circumstances in the sprawling kingdom of Hungary were again different. Despite its distinctive character, the Priory of Hungary did not form a separate langue and instead was part of the German or Italian langues. At the same time

The so-called 'Street of the Knights' in the walled city of Rhodes. This was the most strongly fortified part of the city and was reserved for the Hospitallers, their servants, supporters and guests. The street itself was lined with the auberges or main hostels of the different langues of the Order. (David Nicolle)

RIGHT

After the village of Balsall in the English Midlands, now known as Temple Balsall, was handed over to the Hospitallers on the dissolution of the Military Order of Templars, a fine new church (on the right) was built in local sandstone. The Hospitallers also built a new hall which still survives (on the left), though it has now been converted into houses. (David Nicolle)

OPPOSITE

Part of the Allegory of the Church, a wall-painting made around 1335 by Andrea da Firenze. Amongst the numerous figures are two on the far left who wear the black mantle and white cross of the Hospitallers. The one with a flowing white beard possibly represents the Grand Master Fernandez de Heredia. (in situ, Spanish Chapel, Santa Maria Novella, Florence, Italy/The Bridgeman Art Library)

a large part of the Hungarian state fell within the Priory of Bohemia. The first Hospitaller properties in Hungary had been concentrated in the north-west of the country, but with the acquisition of ex-Templar estates the centre of gravity shifted sharply southwards, beyond the Drava river towards the Adriatic coast of what is now Croatia. Up until the 1330s most of the leading men in the Priory of Hungary had been Italian, but as the indigenous Hungarian aristocracy was increasingly Westernized in culture and attitudes, so it started to take a more active interest in the Order. By the late 14th and 15th centuries most senior Hospitallers in Hungary were themselves Hungarian, and the kings of Hungary tried to play a more direct role in the selection of such senior officers. The situation became so corrupt that in 1448 the Pope tried to get the Hospitallers to reform the Priory of Hungary and end abuses by the local nobility. By this time the Ottoman Turkish advance was getting dangerously close to the Hospitaller preceptories in the south of the kingdom.

The most isolated of all the Hospitaller priories was that of Dacia or Scandinavia. Its lack of communication with both Rome and Rhodes was compounded by the fact that the German Priory tended to act separately from the rest of the Order. Consequently, Hospitaller revenues from its Scandinavian properties rarely reached Rhodes. In 1443 the Order went so far as to consider offering the entire area to the Teutonic Knights in return for a few Teutonic commanderies in Sicily, though this was not actually carried through. There was a similarly notable lack of locally recruited brethren in Denmark, Sweden and Norway.

OPPOSITE

Carvings of heraldic shields flanked by religious figures including the Virgin and Child and St Peter decorated various parts of the fortifications of Bodrum. The upper coat-of-arms is that of the Grand Master Giovanni Battista Orsini (1467–76) while the lower shield is that of a member of the ruling family of the kingdom of Leon and Castile in Spain.(in situ, Bodrum castle; Mary Orr)

DECISION MAKING AND FINANCES

In addition to being a remarkably efficient 'multi-national' organization, the Order of the Hospitallers had an effective system of internal consultation, decision making and justice. It would be wrong to describe it as democratic in the modern sense, because it evolved into a kind of oligarchy dominated by the most experienced men from each langue. Nevertheless legislation within the Order, known as *stabilimenta*, was discussed by the Conventual Chapter, which also acted like a Supreme Court. Those accused of an abuse of authority were called to account in front of their superiors, though the resulting judgements could often be very slow. The senior officers of the Order similarly preferred to consult priories before selecting their own new prior. Following a statute or law drawn up under the Mastership of Philibert de Naillac, and perhaps also reflecting the spread of consultative if not democratic opinion across later medieval Europe, there were more meetings of the Order's Conventual Chapter during the 15th century than ever before. These were held at intervals of one to seven years, usually to discuss pressing matters relating to the papacy, military threats and internal reforms of the Order itself.

On a more day-to-day basis the Order was preoccupied with its finances. Though hugely wealthy it also incurred huge expenses. The cost of buying and transporting food, raw materials, armaments and horses from Western Europe to Rhodes was immense, as previously discussed, as was the cost of building and maintaining the modern fortifications that defended Rhodes. Even as early as 1343 it cost from 800 to 1,000 florins a month to operate an ordinary war-galley. Various modifications were made to the internal financial structure of the Order, not all of which resulted in a greater proportion of revenues going to Rhodes. It therefore became traditional to allow one-fifth of a brother's property to be donated in his will to anyone he chose while the remainder went directly to the Order.

While on one hand the Order often dealt with massive sums of money either being transferred to Rhodes or being invested in Italian banks, on the other hand Hospitaller brethren were concerned with often minor sums. In Rhodes in 1385 a tax on the sale of slaves, soap, wine and other imported goods was sufficient to maintain one 'guard galley' for the island. Twenty-four years later a severe financial crisis in Rhodes was partially alleviated by the arrival of a flotilla of Venetian galleys bringing the huge sum of 5,000 ducats from England, which was at the time one of the most prosperous kingdoms in Christendom. Of this amount, 1,900 ducats were spent on Bodrum castle, 1,000 to pay mercenary troops, 300 on stipends for the brethren and 600 for their *mensa* or food. Other Englishmen offered their *pittance* or small amount, including a certain John Pigot Esquire of York who gave £2 in his will for Bodrum castle's fabric and defence in 1429.

The southern harbour of Lindos, on the western side of the island of Rhodes, was a small but almost perfectly protected natural cove. From here Hospitaller galleys could prey upon Turkish shipping which had little choice but to use the narrow straits between Rhodes and the Anatolian mainland. (David Nicolle)

Just under a century later one of the Hospitallers' largest cargo ships was brought to Rhodes by Father Jacques Gattineau, the Commander of Limoges and Mâcon in France. On board was a collection of extraordinarily rich gifts from the Prior of Provence including an eight-pointed cross of pure gold worth 2,226 gold *ecus de France* and 15 gold medallions each worth 1,000 ecus, excluding the 8,430 ecus paid to the craftsmen who made them. These were intended for display on the altar of the Order's main church in Rhodes and each depicted one of the Fifteen Joys of the Virgin Mary. The same Prior of Provence had earlier sent gilded silver statues of the Twelve Apostles to be ranged along the left and right sides of the high altar, with portable cupboards for when they were not being used, and three solid gold statues of the Lamp of God, the Virgin in Glory, and John the Baptist to be used on the most solemn feast days.

These gifts inspired the Master of the Order himself to purchase a candelabrum supported by silver angels to illuminate the statues. None of these objects are known to survive, but one of the Prior of Provence's gifts was an illuminated missal. Even with its silver box it was only worth 100 ecus but unlike the other magnificent items of gold and silver, this missal still exists in the Library of the Order of St John in London. In addition the Prior of Provence sent more down-to-earth gifts, ranging from four bronze cannon and their carriages costing 2,500 ecus, to 500 shares in the Genoese Bank of St George, worth 9,357 ecus.

The wealth of the Order did not mean that it escaped financial crises. The conquest of Rhodes had been dangerously expensive, resulting in some priories being ordered to limit recruitment and halt all new building operations.

Medical work and the ransoming of prisoners were similarly reduced. Much property was sold, and, despite the acquisition of ex-Templar estates, many Hospitaller houses in Europe remained deep in debt throughout the first half of the 14th century. The Order even had to withdraw from the defence of Izmir on the Anatolian coast when King Edward III defaulted on his debts. The Hospitallers' main Italian bank collapsed and wiped out the Order's huge financial reserve of 360,000 florins (then the dominant coinage in Western Europe).

Under these circumstances it is hardly surprising that the Order undertook major financial reforms. In 1358 the responsibility for the collection of all dues was taken away from priors and placed in the hands of a receiver allocated to each priory. In 1373 a detailed survey of all Hospitaller properties assessed their numbers, values and residents while the baptismal and family names and ages of all presbitors (senior priests), commanders, brethren and donati were recorded. The result made occasionally dismal reading, with diminished incomes,

The 'English Tower' of the Hospitallers' Castle of St Peter at Bodrum was so named because it was largely built with money sent from England during the early 15th century. Support from donors as well as revenues from Hospitaller estates across Europe were vital to finance the Hospitallers' activities, including the building of fortifications in the Aegean region. (David Nicolle)

The fortified walls of Rhodes also protected the city from the sea in case an enemy managed to enter the harbour. Here, however, the defences were weak, old fashioned and lacked the massive artillery bastions which were added to the land walls during the 15th and early 16th centuries. (David Nicolle)

abandoned churches, falling numbers of brethren, too many priests, elderly brothers and absentee preceptors. In northern France, for example, more than half the brethren were priests rather than knights or sergeants. Of the 54 available military brethren nearly three-quarters were over 40 years old and over half were older than 50.

The purge that followed removed many easygoing commandery households, which had already been devastated by the Black Death and other plagues that ravaged Europe in the mid-14th century. This old system of 'families' or households was instead replaced by an efficient new structure in which the commander was often the only 'professed brother' or full member of the Order in each domus. The new system greatly increased the efficiency of raising and of collecting revenues and as a result the amount sent to the central convent in Rhodes almost doubled in the 1370s and 1380s.

Tensions between the langues were more difficult to resolve and the solutions sometimes reflected a shift in political power within the Order rather than anything else. For example a decline in the power of the Provençals resulted in their langues being reunited in the mid-15th century and thus losing their double vote in the Conventual Chapter. Instead the langue of Spain was divided into two, so gaining a double vote.

In 1410 a Chapter General of the Order, held at Aix in southern France rather than in Rhodes, resulted in further much-needed reforms, mostly to remove fraud, restore the authority of the Master and attempt to ensure that brethren obeyed the original statutes of their Order. The Chapter General also looked at individual and financial quarrels, breaches of discipline, usurpations and failures of duty. More detailed decisions resulted in the Admiral being ordered to draw up a register of sailors and to divide them into companies sufficient to crew one galley. Problems of payment for garrisons on Lango and elsewhere were considered. The Turcopolier was ordered to stop making 'mutations' or changes of personnel amongst the turcopoles without the Master's or Council's authorization; and it was decided that the Prior of Aquitaine should be allowed ten horses while the Prior of Champagne should have only eight. Such varied considerations, from the wide-ranging to the highly specific, were characteristic of medieval administration, not only that of the Hospitallers.

Another perhaps much-needed reform concerned the Order's statutes themselves. These had increased in number over the centuries, resulting in confusion, disagreement and occasional contradiction. So the revised statutes of 1447 and 1489 were arranged systematically. Then there was the vexed question of language. The Hospitallers' original 12th-century statutes were written in Provençal but in 1357 they had been translated into Latin, which was understood throughout Europe and could be more easily translated into other languages. In 1493 the revised statutes were again drawn up in Latin and it was not until 1567 that Italian became the official language of the Order.

Recruitment, Discipline, Training and Daily Life

WHO BECAME A HOSPITALLER?

The Military Orders, including the Hospitallers, recruited from essentially the same groups. Military casualties and death from disease meant that new recruits were constantly needed and plenty wanted to join the Hospitallers. In the early days the main difficulty was the Hospitaller Order's shortage of money and in this context it is worth noting that the Order in the Holy Land sent back to Europe more requests for matériel than for men. Those who were sent to the Middle East naturally tended to be fit and relatively young while older members of the Order generally remained in Europe, administering and where necessary protecting the fast-expanding support network of priories and commanderies.

During the 12th and early 13th centuries most brethren of the Hospitaller Order were not recruited from the nobility but came from all free members of society, including serfs who had obtained manumission from their feudal lords. Plenty of fighting men wanted to go on crusade, but those who did so had to have sufficient disposable income to pay their own costs. Cavalry warfare was expensive, so that even the so-called 'poor knights' must still have been wealthy compared to peasants.

The first recorded restrictions on entry date from 1262 and 1270, after which preference was given to men of knightly rank. They, of course, generally brought larger financial donations with them at a time when the Order was getting short of money. Thereafter restrictions on recruitment became ever stricter. During the 13th century it became necessary for a brother-knight to be of knightly descent and the evidence shows that the majority of such men came from the lower aristocracy, ordinary knights or *ministeriales* (elite warriors of serf status).

France remained the powerhouse of the crusading movement, at least of crusades to the Middle and Near East, while also providing the bulk of Hospitaller

OPPOSITE
Crusaders massacring the Muslim inhabitants of Antioch in a late 13th-century manuscript made in what remained of the Crusader States. The central figure seems to have an early form of the arms of the Order of Hospitallers on his shield, though this probably merely identifies him as a Christian knight. (Histoire Universelle, f.43v, MS. 142, Bibliothèque Municipale, Boulogne, France)

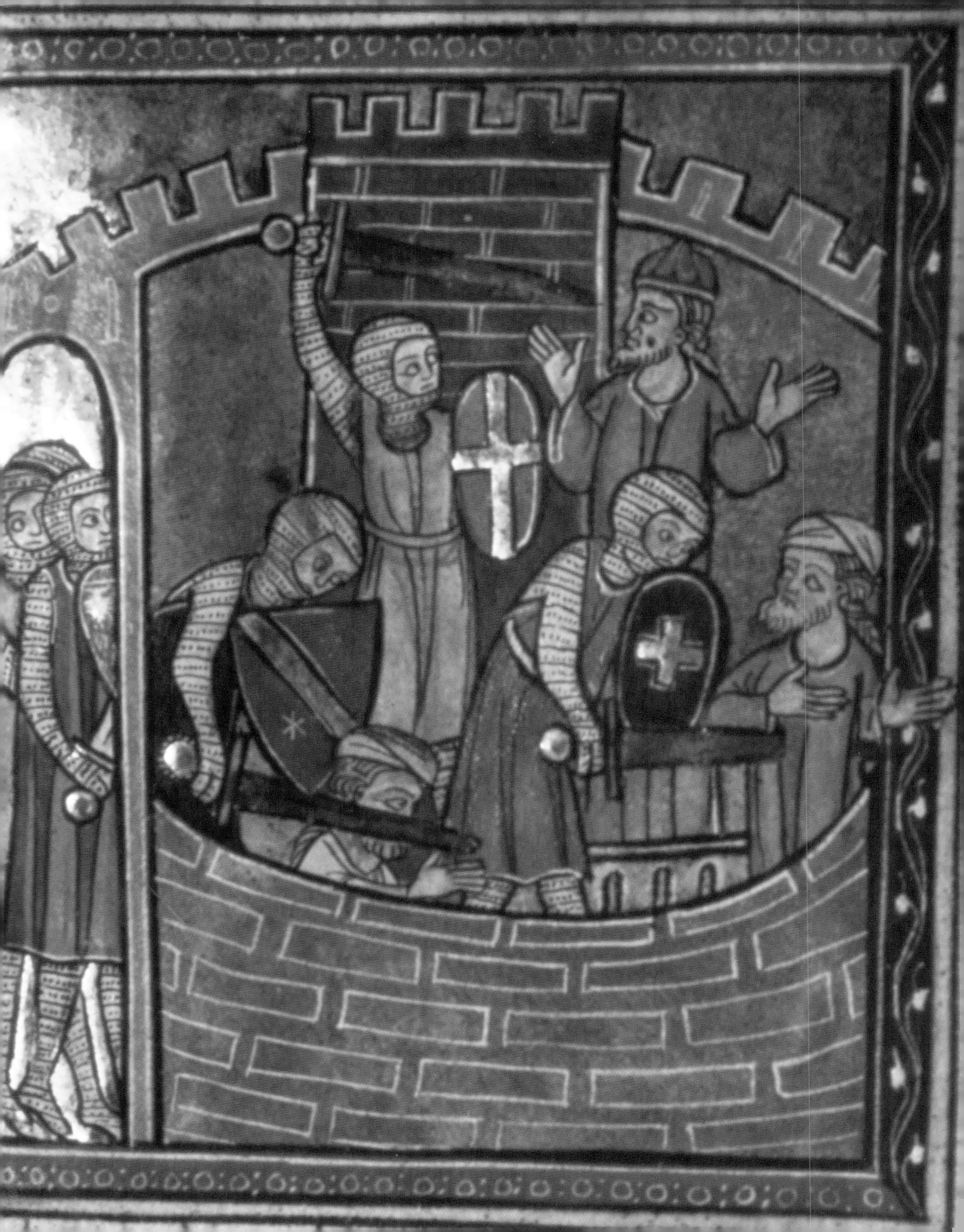

This southern French carved capital is believed to be the oldest surviving three-dimensional medieval European representation of a crossbow. When it was made in the very late 11th century, the crossbow was regarded as a wicked weapon used by demons, as shown here, and by Muslims. Christians were not supposed to use it against each other though they could employ it against infidels. (in situ, cathedral of St Sernin, Toulouse, France; David Nicolle)

personnel. From the later 11th century until well into the 14th century the reputation of French knights was higher than those of any other country, the prowess of the northern French being considered greater than that of the southern French. This French domination was also reflected in the fact that of the 13 langues of the later 13th-century Order of Hospitallers, three came from France. As just one small example of this French preponderance, over half the Hospitaller brethren in Cyprus in 1302 similarly came from France.

From 1066 onwards and throughout much of the 14th century England was, in terms of its aristocracy and general culture, a 'colony' of France. This meant that English recruits to the Hospitallers were very similar to their French cousins, though they did have their own langue. During the 12th and 13th centuries the Anglo-Norman aristocracy of England largely spoke French. Anglo-Normans played a particularly significant role during the 12th century, despite the steady demilitarization of the English knightly class that began in the mid-12th century as the knights began to transform into archetypal English 'squires'.

A remarkably large number of troops was available in the German Empire where the concept of military service to God was deeply rooted in the system of ministeriales and *riters* (knights, literally 'riders') who themselves evolved into Germany's *milites Christi* or 'Knights of Christ'. Ministeriales were originally unfree serfs, who only came to be recognized as part of the nobility during the 12th century. In Germany and the German-dominated neighbouring regions of Central Europe, recruitment for the Hospitallers and Templars faced stiff competition from the locally based Order of Teutonic Knights. While there was reluctance to join the largely French Templars, who were also considered too close to the papacy at a time when the German emperor and Roman popes were often at loggerheads, the Hospitallers did not face the same degree of resistance. They seem to have recruited with particular success in Bohemia, though most of the known priors, or leaders of priory provinces in this part of Europe, were of German origin.

The Order similarly flourished in Hungary, which was often closely linked to the Hospitaller administrative structure in Italy. Here most of the Hospitallers' leading men were of French or Italian origin, while the ordinary brothers were largely Hungarians or German settlers. The Hungarian nobility itself tended not to become involved with the Order, perhaps because the indigenous aristocracy was still largely non-feudal and reflected an earlier, tribal social structure. Noble families owned their lands freehold rather than as feudal fiefs and estates could not be given away, even to a religious order, without the consent of the

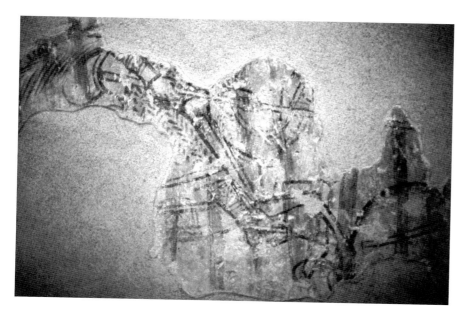

The fragmentary late 12th- or early 13th-century wall-paintings at Aquileia in north-eastern Italy are particularly interesting because they show weapons and military equipment that had more in common with the neighbouring Balkans than with the rest of Italy. For example, the mailed horsemen shown here wields his spear with two hands. (in situ, Crypt of Massenzio, cathedral, Aquileia, Italy; David Nicolle)

family as a whole. As a result most of the land that the Hospitallers did acquire in Hungary came from widows and those without heirs.

During this period the kingdom of Croatia was under the crown of Hungary, and once again most of its leading Hospitallers appear to have come from France or Italy. Local men from Croatia and Bosnia did join the Order and they were in turn found serving in Italy or even as the commanders of Hospitaller ships. Meanwhile Italy was something of a special case. Like Germany, it had abundant well-trained professional soldiers of all ranks, but their interests tended to focus upon local and usually secular affairs rather than the crusading movement or the Military Orders.

In the Iberian peninsula religious motivation and enthusiasm for war against Muslims was high but for obvious reasons focussed on the local frontier with al-Andalus, the 'Moorish' Islamic southern part of the peninsula. However, senior Hospitallers in what became Spain and Portugal were largely of local origin and many were from humble backgrounds. Perhaps for these reasons the Iberian Hospitallers, like the members of other Military Orders in this region, seem not to have had that uncomprehending hatred of Islam that initially characterized the Military Orders in the Holy Land.

The numbers of recruits varied over the years. Paradoxically, there seem to have been too many aspirants in the later 13th century when the Crusader States were in deep crisis and the Military Orders might have been expected to welcome as many new members as possible. On this occasion the problem again seems to have been financial and despite its proverbial wealth the Order of the Hospitallers, like the Order of the Temple, could not afford to maintain as many fighting men or as many great castles as it might have liked. In the early days any Hospitaller commander could accept a knight as a recruit, though only the Master of the Order or perhaps a specially designated brother could accept a sergeant. In 1270 it was decided that the authority of the Master was needed before the less important Middle Eastern commanders of Cyprus, Tripoli and Armenia could create new brethren of the Order. The commanders and chapters of the larger establishments at Acre, Crac des Chevaliers and Marqab could, however, still accept such recruits.

In 1292, a year after the fall of Acre, there once again seem to have been too many brother-knights in relation to the Hospitallers' now strained finances. As a result no new brothers could be created anywhere, except in Spain where there might have been a local shortage, without a specific licence from the Master or the Grand Commander who was now based in Cyprus. It is also possible that some of the knightly refugees from the Crusader States wanted to join the Order after they had lost their estates on the mainland, since many no longer had any means of maintaining themselves.

OPPOSITE
The Hospitaller Grand Master Pierre d'Aubusson instructing his subordinates during the unsuccessful Ottoman siege of Rhodes in 1480. (Obsidionis Rhodie Urbis Descriptio by William Caoursin, f.33v, MS. Lat. 6067, Bibliothèque Nationale, Paris, France; The Bridgeman Art Library)

JOINING THE ORDER

During the 12th century the system of child oblation, or attachment to the Order as novitiates, was considerably more important than it would be in later years. Such novitiates included abandoned children and although they were not officially obliged to join the Order once they came of age, there was probably some pressure to do so. At what precise age a child novitiate became a Hospitaller brother is unfortunately unknown. In some other Orders it was at 14 or 15 years old and by the early 13th century a recruit may normally have spent three years as a novitiate. Heavy casualties during the 13th century may by then have contributed to a decline in the enlistment of young novitiates. Not only were parents unwilling to send their sons to probable death but the Order may have preferred men who were already of military age or who had already acquired military skills. On the downside, an absence of a proper novitiate system led to widespread illiteracy amongst recruits and frequent breaches in regulations that were not fully understood even by fully fledged brethren of the Order.

Less is known about the individual motivation of recruits to the Hospitaller Order. The life of a brother was said to be hard, but may often have looked relatively easy to someone on the outside. There was also the increased status of being a Hospitaller, as well as certain career prospects. Joining a Military Order similarly meant less 'abandonment of the world' than did joining a non-military, monastic order.

Some recruits may actually have been looking for martyrdom in war against Islam at a time of genuine religious fervour, though this seems to have been more characteristic of the 12th than the 13th century. In the late 13th century a few recruits seem to have been trying to escape debt or legal punishment, though it was strictly against the Order's rules to accept such men. In 1236, for example, King Henry III of England allowed Geoffrey Bauzan, a prisoner in the Tower of London, to join the Hospitallers on condition that he did not return to England without permission from the king. The Church similarly wanted Count Raymond of Toulouse, who was accused of sheltering the Albigensian heretics, to enter the Hospitallers or the Templars as part of a peace agreement to end the Albigensian Crusade, though he refused.

All recruits had to be free, of legitimate birth, healthy, spiritually clean and free from debt. There was no fixed lower age limit, though there were rules about when a man could become a brother-knight or be ordained a brother-priest. Married men were only accepted if their living spouses agreed. There were occasions when man and wife joined together, though they would promptly be separated. Men were expected to be fit enough to fight, though standards dropped in times of crisis. Ex-members of other religious orders were not accepted, since the Rules of the Military Orders were considered to be easier than those of

A Venetian pilgrim galley outside the harbour of Rhodes, in a 15th-century Italian wood engraving. The long row of windmills on the harbour mole was one of the most distinctive features of Rhodes, and a few of them still stand. (Roger-Viollet/TopFoto)

regular monastic orders, nor were Hospitallers permitted to leave once they had joined. A few cases are known where men transferred from one Military Order to another, but this was generally frowned upon.

Sometimes an individual managed to buy his way past these regulations and into the Order. However, if knowledge of this venality became too public it tended to result in a scandal, as happened at the Hospitaller convent of Fürstenfeld in Styria in 1278. It was normal for recruits to the Military Orders to be expected to provide their own clothing and equipment, for example at the Hospitaller convent at Siguena in Aragon in 1227 when a man came with his own horse, clothing and bed 'as decreed in the Order of the Hospital'.

Taking the Habit

The entry procedure was relatively simple, though solemn. A recruit was warned that 'although it may be that you see us well-clothed and with fine horses, and think that we have every comfort, you would be mistaken, for when you would like to eat, it will be necessary to fast. And when you want to sleep, it will be necessary to keep watch.' The acceptance of a new brother involved a ceremony similar to that of a feudal investiture and took place during the Sunday chapter or meeting of a convent. There the aspirant would ask the Master of the Order or the presiding brother for membership. The president of the meeting then asked the chapter if they agreed. If a majority did so, then the candidate would be asked several questions: had he asked to enter another Order, was he married, in debt, or a serf to any lord? If he was found to have lied he would 'lose the habit' or in other words be expelled. A missal was then brought forward. The candidate placed his hands on the book and swore an oath to God, the Virgin Mary and St John the Baptist, stating that he would live and die in obedience to the sovereign given him by God – in other words the Master of the Order – in chastity, without property, to be a serf and slave of 'his lords the sick'.

In return the Order then promised him bread, water and humble clothing. He took the missal into the chapel and placed it on the altar, then took it back to the president who held up a mantle, the basic garment of the Order, and said 'Behold this, the sign of the Cross, which you will wear on this mantle in remembrance of Him who suffered death and passion on the Cross for you and for us other sinners. May God, by the Cross and by the vow of obedience that you have made in faith and in deed, keep you and defend you now and for ever, from the power of the Devil.' The mantle was placed upon the new brother's shoulders and he was given the kiss of peace, which he then exchanged with all brethren present. Henceforth the recruit could not return to secular life. His family did, however, gain spiritual benefit from his membership of the Order of St John of the Hospital of Jerusalem.

Brother-Sergeants

The recruitment of brother-sergeants was somewhat different. Amongst the Hospitallers the brethren initially consisted of brothers-at-office and brothers-at-labour, there apparently being no distinction in the earliest years between brother-knights and brother-sergeants. All were merely brethren. However, brother-sergeants were first mentioned as a separate group in 1206 and thereafter were always fewer than the brother-knights. During the 13th century, Hospitaller sergeants were divided into brother-sergeants-at-arms who were soldiers, and brother-sergeants-at-service who generally undertook menial or administrative tasks under the authority of the Grand Commander.

The now battered 15th-century statues representing the Virgin Mary, centre, flanked by perhaps St John on the left and a Grand Master of the Order of the Hospitallers on the right, can still be seen inside the Gate of St John. This is still one of the main entrances through the southern wall of the fortified city of Rhodes. (David Nicolle)

Like the brother-knights they lived a conventual or community life and were often given considerable responsibility. Some brethren-at-arms became brethren-at-service, perhaps as a result of age or declining health, but there was no known movement in the other direction. Positions of senior rank were sometimes given to such men from non-knightly backgrounds, though this was a feature of areas away from the war-torn frontiers and more especially in Western Europe, where sergeants played a significant role. Nor must they be confused with the much larger number of sergeants who were not brethren but were merely servants of the Order.

Information about the backgrounds of these brother-sergeants is extremely limited. Most seem to have been of peasant or craftsman origin and very few ever seem to have been serfs, because a serf needed to be granted his freedom before he could enter a religious order. Nevertheless, there were examples throughout Western Christendom where feudal lords offered their serfs freedom if the latter wanted to enter the religious life. There were also a few cases where men from knightly families joined the Order as brother-sergeants, perhaps because they had not yet been knighted or came from families that could no longer afford a proper knightly role. In reality, the forces that the Hospitallers could field were both varied and relatively few in number. This variety may have helped the Military Orders lead the way in terms of military specialization by different types of troops or men trained in particular military skills.

RECRUITMENT IN LATER CENTURIES

Recruitment to the Order of Hospitallers from the 14th to mid-16th centuries was based upon essentially the same principles and systems as had been the case in the 12th and 13th centuries. However, the world from which these men were drawn was itself changing and this was inevitably reflected in Hospitaller recruitment. Given the changes within the knightly elite, added to what seems to have been a notable crisis of identity and excessive numbers of men compared to women in some parts of Europe, the motivation of recruits to the Hospitaller Order is liable to have been very mixed.

There were also other factors at work. The dissolution of the Templars provided the Hospitallers with greatly increased wealth but not recruits. In fact ex-Templars were obliged to join another religious order, but were forbidden to enter that of the Hospitallers. Enthusiasm for crusading had declined sharply, which not only reduced the flow of recruits but also had an effect upon the donation of land and other assets.

Somewhat hysterical calls for crusade by scholars who spread horror stories about the cruelty and military effectiveness of the 'terrible Turk' may actually have backfired in terms of recruitment to Military Orders such as the Hospitallers. The Church sometimes tried to counter this propaganda by saying that the infidel foe was not as invincible as was so widely believed, but its reassurances largely appear to have been ignored. In this situation the small Hospitaller outpost on Rhodes almost seemed like an irrelevance and it was not until its defeat of a major Ottoman attack in 1480 that the Order saw a significant increase in recruitment.

Before that notable victory, many of the men who joined the Hospitallers may have done so to find a career rather than as a result of crusading fervour. Certainly the Order came to be seen as a good career opportunity. Some parents apparently pushed younger sons into an organization that required no educational qualifications, though there is no evidence that it was used as a refuge for the dim-witted or as yet to raise a family's prestige. There continued to be little scope for religious contemplation within the Order of the Hospitallers and, apart from a small number of men who were sent on rotation to Rhodes, little scope for military action either. The Hospitallers' charitable medical work had by now declined in importance and there was little communal religious life in widely scattered Hospitaller houses where there were often only a handful of professed brethren.

For most brethren, both knights and sergeants, life in the Order was one of perhaps tedious administrative work, but it was secure and it offered status in a society where such things were highly valued. Even in Rhodes life was generally quiet and offered less opportunity for adventure than, for example, the warlike Baltic outposts of the rival Order of Teutonic Knights. Furthermore Rhodes was so distant, so expensive to reach and in which to live once men had arrived, that the Hospitallers often discouraged brethren from going there unless they could afford their own passage, military equipment and horses.

During the 12th and 13th centuries the Order of the Hospitallers had largely been dominated by men from southern France, from what became the Priory of Saint-Gilles or Provence. Frenchmen, including those from the centre and north of the country, continued to dominate the Order throughout most of the 14th century. Information on the numbers of brethren in the central convent, initially in Cyprus and then in Rhodes, from 1302 to 1522 shows only small numbers from England and Germany. Most were still from France though in later years the numbers from Spain and Italy did increase. In addition there were a few from Portugal, Scotland, Denmark and Hungary. Rivalry between the langues within the Order was reflected within Europe, as when the Priory of Provence annexed that of Navarre and sought to dominate those of southern Italy and Hungary. Eventually the way in which Master Roger de Pins used his position to advance his own nation became so blatant that the Chapter General, which was effectively the supreme council of the Order of Hospitallers, insisted on urgent reforms. These led, in 1374, to the election of the first non-Provençal Master for 78 years. Unfortunately it was then followed by a comparable period during which men of Spanish origin almost took over the Order.

The Hospitallers continued to face different problems of recruitment in different countries. In England, for example, the 14th and 15th centuries saw widespread anti-papal feeling because the popes were seen as pro-French during the Hundred Years' War, and to some extent this resentment rubbed off on the Hospitallers. During this period most English brethren came from the Midlands and northern England, largely being drawn from those of the minor knightly class and what was emerging as the typically English 'rural squires'.

The inner moat of the Hospitaller castle of Crac des Chevaliers, which is originally believed to have extended around more of the inner citadel, rather than being filled at the south-western corner as seen here. It also served as a vital store of washing and perhaps even drinking water, at least for the animals housed in huge stables just to the left of this photograph. (David Nicolle)

The massive Hospitaller castle of Marqab, on the left of the fortified hilltop in this photograph, was only a small part of what became an extensive site during crusader times. Spreading northward, to the right in this picture, was a large and strongly fortified town which was practically deserted after the population migrated to the flourishing nearby port city of Banyas. (David Nicolle)

The Hospitallers' situation differed yet again in the later medieval Slav lands and Hungary. In the latter kingdom, Western-style feudal structures were still a relatively new introduction and there continued to be widespread resentment amongst the indigenous aristocracies against the influence wielded by foreign, largely German and Italian, Hospitaller elites. Both factors inhibited local recruitment. In Italy relations between Venice and the Hospitallers, who had fundamentally different attitudes towards dealings with the Islamic world, still meant that very few Venetians joined the Order.

Meanwhile in the Iberian peninsula the Hospitallers continued to face competition from local Spanish Military Orders for recruits, donations and royal patronage. In earlier years most Iberian Hospitallers seem to have been of non-noble origin but there was a clear process of what might be called aristocratization during the 14th century, particularly amongst those holding high office in the Iberian priories. The result was eventually a shocking degree of nepotism amongst senior Hospitallers drawn from the Iberian aristocracies, particularly in Portugal. Though entry into the Order in Spain and Portugal apparently remained open, access to the most prestigious and thus lucrative offices was soon almost monopolized by a few noble families which, in the later 14th century, also rose to prominence in the Order outside Spain.

As already stated, the process of admission into the Order remained theoretically much as it had been before. Until the system was reformed, the heads of local convents could admit recruits under strict limitations. Novitiates and those donati who were awaiting admission as novitiates still lived in Hospitaller houses, though as the size of the Order's communities in Europe declined, a larger proportion of brother knights spent their novitiate in Rhodes itself. Here the Order faced different manpower problems, not necessarily concerned with Hospitaller brethren. During the mid-14th century there were so few 'Latins' or legally recognized men of European origin in the islands that

The castle of Qala'at Ahmur, 'Red Castle' or Castel Rouge as it was known in crusader times, was one of the Hospitallers' smaller fortifications in this fertile but vulnerable part of Syria. It has a single corner tower, the rest of the castle consisting of a central keep directly linked to the outer walls on three sides plus a small courtyard on the fourth. (David Nicolle)

the Chapter ruled that those with Latin fathers but Greek mothers should be considered legally Latin. In 1424 Latins resident in Rhodes were also allowed to enter the Order, if they obtained letters of naturalization from their parents' home states back in Europe, a requirement that would seem to have excluded second-generation settlers. In 1478 some local Rhodian Greeks requested permission to enter but this was denied on the grounds that it would have been against the Hospitallers' original statutes.

The process of initiation into the Order had changed little, as shown in a detailed description of the admission of King Jaime II of Aragon's eldest son, also named Jaime, in 1319. He, incidentally, was escaping an unwanted marriage.

During this church service Father Arnau de Soler, the Preceptor of Barcelona and Aliaga, sat before the altar holding the Gospels and a cross. Jaime, dressed as a Hospitaller but without the characteristic *clamida* or mantle, knelt before him, placing his hands on the book and cross. Father Arnau gave the normal explanation and said that the new entrant would have a probationary year. After making his vows of obedience Jaime rose, and placed the book and cross on Arnau's knees. The preceptor then received him as a brother, placing the black mantle with its white cross across his shoulders, whereupon all the brethren present knelt to pray for their new Hospitaller brother. New brethren were normally assigned a residence in a house under the preceptor's obedience and were often allotted a squire, two servants, a horse and a pack-animal.

Brother-knights had always been more influential in meetings of the central convent, or in other local chapters, than were other Hospitaller brethren, but as the Order became more aristocratic so their voices became even louder. This upward mobility was seen in a statute that defined the number of noble quarterings in a coat-of-arms that an aspiring brother-knight needed. In Italy it was only four because many decades of intermarriage between noble and wealthy bourgeoisie families in this urban and economically highly developed country made it unwise to look too deeply into a young aristocrat's origins. In France and Spain eight noble quarterings would be required, whereas in Germany it was now no fewer than 16. Even the illegitimate sons of rulers were excluded in Germany, though they were admitted to other langues. Such rules were taken very seriously and for a family to have a member refused entry was a blow to its honour. Recruitment to the Order of Hospitallers became yet more selective and aristocratic after 1565, with a concern not only for several generations of the purest noble blood but also that there should be no taint of heresy in the aftermath of the Reformation.

THE HOSPITALLERS AND NON-BRETHREN

On the margins of the Order of the Hospitallers were a variety of other groups, several of whom have already been mentioned. These included the donati who, since the 12th century, consisted of noblemen who wanted to join as full brethren. They had to wait in a sort of queue, many having gone to the Middle East at their own expense. During the 13th century an extraordinary form of comic ceremony developed to accompany the proper religious ceremony when such a donat became a full brother. The reasons for this are obscure, but a new recruit would be dressed in comical, almost ridiculous, costume and be accompanied in procession from the Baths of St John in Acre to the Hospitaller compound to the sound of drums and trumpets. Such buffoonery was, however, forbidden in 1270.

RIGHT

The siege of Antioch was a particularly popular subject in illustrated medieval accounts of the crusades. This example was made in Acre in the late 13th century and includes a fine portrayal of a man-powered stone-throwing mangonel operated by a team of armoured men. (William of Tyre's History of Outremer, *f.33r, MS. 828, Bibliothèque Municipale, Lyon, France; akg-images/Erich Lessing)*

OPPOSITE

*King Louis IX of France leaves Aigues Mortes, in an Italian-style manuscript which is believed to have been made in Acre in 1290, a year before that city fell to the Mamluks. In cultural terms the remnants of the Crusader States now had more in common with Italy than with France, and this is reflected in the armour given to King Louis and his army in this picture, as well as the accurate representations of ships below. (*History of Outremer, *f.336v, MS. Plut. LXI, 10, Biblioteca Medicea-Laurenziana, Florence, Italy)*

The *confraters* were ordinary laymen who were associated with the Hospitallers but did not normally become brethren. They were first mentioned in 1111 and eventually included the most senior noblemen of the Crusader States, such as the Count of Tripoli and the Prince of Antioch. Eventually even the kings of France and Aragon were counted amongst their number. Such confraters agreed to defend a Hospitaller convent or house and were admitted to their status by a simple religious ceremony at the altar or merely at the door of a Hospitaller church. During the 13th century a separate Confraternity of St George and St Belian was established for Christians of the Melkite Syrian Church, which was in communion with Rome, and this was closely associated with the Order of Hospitallers.

As a proper religious Order, the Hospitallers needed their own priests, though the first confirmed reference to such a clerical brother only dates from 1154. Thereafter the Order continued to face difficulties in recruiting enough priests into its ranks and many Hospitaller houses did not have resident priests or even chaplains. Instead, outsiders were brought in to serve the brothers' spiritual needs.

There is considerable doubt about the dating of the carved corbels, mostly in the form of armoured knights, which support the restored roof of the early 14th-century Hospitaller church at Temple Balsall in the English Midlands. They may be early Victorian additions to the structure, or Victorian replacements of now lost and perhaps damaged medieval carvings, or they may be 'tidied up' originals. In the opinion of the author the second possibility seems most likely. (in situ, parish church, Temple Balsall, England; David Nicolle)

Ordinary sergeants rather than brother-sergeants first appeared in Hospitaller sources in 1182 and included ordinary servants. Most seem to have been contracted to serve for one year. They ate separately from the brethren but included personnel who performed essential functions such as scribes, public notaries, advocates, doctors, chamberlains, chamber-pages, pack drivers, cooks, kitchen boys, butlers, barbers, farriers, footmen and mercenary soldiers. The grooms who looked after horses and the squires or *scutifers* who looked after arms and armour were particularly important. A regulation issued in 1302 stated that every brother-knight was allowed two and each brother-sergeant one; this arrangement had probably been in place for many years. The medical staff who actually looked after the sick or injured in the Hospitallers' various hospitals were not brethren of the Order.

As already stated, the backbone of Hospitaller power was financial rather than military. By the later 12th century the Order held large territories in the Crusader States and Europe. Those in the Middle East included feudal fiefs, or estates, where feudal vassals owed the Order military service. But only one such Middle Eastern fief is known to have been an ordinary 'landed fief' as known in Western Europe. The rest were various forms of money or bezant fiefs, which produced revenues to support a knight. These were nevertheless supposed to contribute knights and other troops to the Hospitaller muster. Unfortunately the reliability of such Hospitaller vassals was not necessarily high, especially as many of the latter were indigenous Arabs. Their numbers are unknown and there is little hard evidence that local communities gave military support to Hospitaller castle garrisons. Such direct local support was, in fact, more characteristic of Hospitaller castles and fiefs in the Iberian peninsula than in the Holy Land.

Local, regional or indigenous troops did, however, play a significant role in Hospitaller forces as turcopoles. Their origins and even their military equipment varied. Some were almost certainly captured Muslim soldiers who had converted to Christianity and continued to serve in the same manner as they had in Islamic armies. Clearly not all were horse-archers and many appear to have fought as infantry. Some appear to have been recruited from the indigenous Arab Christian population, from the Armenians and from men of mixed European settler and local origin. They were placed under the Turcopolier who was only appointed as and when needed. Turcopoles were stationed at Bayt Jibrin in 1179 and in Acre in 1258 where they had held their own quarters since 1206. They may have become the largest group of mercenaries in the Hospitaller army.

Even less is known about 14th- and 15th-century turcopoles than those of the previous period. Many of the turcopoles who fought for the king of Cyprus were recruited from the indigenous Greeks and perhaps more recently arrived Syrian Christian or Armenian communities. The same is likely to have been true of Hospitaller turcopoles in and around Rhodes. It is, however, clear that amongst non-Latin troops, non-Greeks were regarded as more reliable than Greeks. These included Arab Christians descended from families who had fled from Syria with the collapse of the Crusader States in the late 13th century. Amongst them, the Arab Maronite Christians of Syria and Lebanon came to be seen as a sort of non-Latin military elite.

The distinction between the turcopoles and other locally recruited Christian mercenaries is not entirely clear, though both groups were controlled and led by European or 'Frankish' officers who were not necessarily full Hospitaller brethren. Armenians were considered reliable, Syriac Jacobites less so though this did not mean that Jacobites were less warlike. Around Malatya, just north of the northernmost crusader outposts, Syriac Jacobite monasteries apparently recruited garrisons from amongst their local co-religionists. In what is now Lebanon, the Maronite Christians were regarded as the most reliable of all local recruits because their Church accepted union with the Latin Church of Rome, while in Palestine Christians were again a substantial minority, though most were from the Greek or Orthodox Church.

Clearly the Hospitallers were enlisting paid Western European mercenaries by the early 13th century, most perhaps being crossbowmen. Such professional soldiers had been taking an increasingly prominent role in Western European armies during the 12th century and similarly became a vital part of the forces of the Crusader States in the Middle East. Their wages were quite high when

The ordinary working men who produced the food and wealth which ultimately financed both the Military Orders and the crusading movement are only rarely shown in medieval art as respected members of society. However, their labour was often honoured symbolically, for example in this 15th- or 16th-century Norman French wooden carving on the exterior of a building, where an unnamed saint rests his hand upon a spade, the symbol of hard agricultural labour. (in situ, 28 rue de Tanniers, Verneuil, France; David Nicolle)

The small island of Tilos in the south-eastern part of the Aegean Sea was one of the Hospitallers' less important possessions. However, it still needed to be protected and as a result Tilos had at least three castles. That of Agriosikia, seen here, served as a place of refuge for the local population in case of enemy – usually Turkish – attack. (Bob Rankin)

compared to other jobs available to men of free but non-knightly origin, and they were present in large numbers amongst the nominally Hospitaller forces that defended Acre during the final siege of 1291.

Hospitaller brother knights would also have served alongside, and often probably commanded, the large numbers of European mercenary soldiers who came to Rhodes on short-term contracts. These were found to be essential following the failure of the Order's attempts to establish an effective Western European feudal military settler population in Rhodes.

The sisters of the Order of St John of the Hospital originally seem to have been little more than female servants, including those who looked after sick female pilgrims in the hospital in Jerusalem. Many women apparently wanted to join the Order, perhaps because its Rule was relatively easy and existing nunneries were both few in number and exclusive in their intake. The Hospitallers similarly came to favour female recruits from the feudal elite and nobility. Eventually entry for sisters seems to have become even more exclusive than for brother-knights.

Some documents seem to indicate that bedouin tribes of frontier regions could be regarded as 'vassals' of a Military Order. In February 1179, for example, the turcopoles of the Hospitaller garrison at Bayt Jibrin were accused of 'plundering of the bedouin of the Temple'. Presumably these bedouin had some sort of protection agreement with the Templars or Hospitallers, perhaps in return for acting as guides and agreeing not to raid settled regions owned by the Military Orders themselves. Perhaps these bedouin also exchanged their leather, livestock and horses in return for cereals, clothing and manufactured goods from the Hospitallers or Templars, just as they had done with previous Islamic authorities.

A comparable arrangement probably existed between the Hospitallers and the Isma'ilis or so-called 'Assassins' of the Syrian coastal mountains. The latter were Shi'a Muslims of a distinctive sect and as such were regarded as heretics by their Sunni Muslim neighbours. Perhaps they accepted some sort of theoretical Hospitaller suzerainty as a form of insurance policy. Some Isma'ili-held castles clearly paid tribute to the Hospitallers at various times, though there were also significant disagreements.

Although the primitive wall-paintings in the castle at Avio in northern Italy have no connection with the Hospitallers, they provide some of the best illustrations of tactics and military training during this period. They were painted around 1340 and here the crossbowmen who skirmish with the enemy are protected by the shield-bearing pavesarii carrying large mantlet shields. Behind them comes the main force of infantrymen. (in situ, Castel Sabbionara, Avio, Italy; David Nicolle)

HOSPITALLER CAREERS

The careers of leading figures within the Order shed light on the origins of its upper echelons. Philibert de Naillac, for example, commanded the Hospitaller contingent during the disastrous Crusade of Nicopolis in 1396. His family was one of the oldest in the Berry region and amongst the most important in western France, playing a notable role during the Hundred Years' War. Philibert's brother, Guillaume II 'Le Preux', was seigneur of Naillac castle, Le Blanc, Chateaubrun, and served as the seneschal or governor of Guyenne for King Charles V of France against the English. Meanwhile Philibert became Grand Prior of the Hospitallers in Aquitaine, and was then selected as the 33rd Grand Master of the Order. After surviving the catastrophic Crusade of Nicopolis, he commanded a small fleet in the Aegean and Mediterranean, which continued to give the Ottomans a great deal of trouble, as well as raiding the coasts of the Mamluk Sultanate in Lebanon. He eventually died in 1421, to be succeeded as Master of the Hospitallers by Antonio de Fluvia.

Aleman de Rochechenard, the hugely wealthy Prior of Provence in the early 16th century, had fought in defence of Rhodes in 1480 and still commanded Hospitaller galleys several decades later. In England Father Robert Hales took part in the appalling sack of Alexandria in 1365 and then became Prior of England

A carved wooden panel from Lebanon, perhaps originally from an Armenian church, and probably dating from the late 13th or 14th century. The mounted archer with a trained hunting cat on the rump of his horse was a popular motif in western Asian and Middle Eastern art, though it was also seen in parts of Eastern and Central Europe. In fact this figure could be seen as representing the local turcopole troops who played such a vital role in medieval Hospitaller forces. (ex-Pharaon Collection, present whereabouts unknown; Erica Dodd)

where, however, he was beheaded after having unsuccessfully attempted to introduce a poll tax as Royal Treasurer. Another Englishman, Father Peter Hold, was recorded as commander of the strategic mainland fortress of Bodrum in 1412.

In early 14th-century Germany a brother-knight, Father Berthold von Henneberg, was the Hospitaller lieutenant in Polonia while his brother by birth governed their family estates in Franconia. Together they dabbled in imperial politics as counsellors to the King-Emperor Henry VII. Meanwhile one of their cousins, Father Albrecht von Schwarzburg, had helped conquer Rhodes. He was made Grand Preceptor in 1312 and was sent to Rome to negotiate the transfer of ex-Templar properties to the Hospitallers. As Grand Preceptor Father Albrecht also commanded the 24 ships, 80 Hospitaller brethren and other secular knights who inflicted defeats upon Turkish naval squadrons in 1318 and 1319.

In the Iberian peninsula Father Alfonso Ortiz, the Prior of Castile, was less successful as a naval commander. He led a combined Christian fleet to crushing defeat by Moroccan galleys off Algeciras in 1340, partly due to the Muslim crews' superior seamanship and archery but also as a result of the Moroccan commander Muhammad 'Alah Azafi's superior tactical skill. Perhaps the most famous of all medieval Iberian Hospitallers was Juan Fernandez de Heredia. He was of noble origin, became a brother-knight in 1328, and earned a reputation not only as a highly efficient administrator but also as a skilled diplomat. De Heredia became a close friend of the heir to the Aragonese throne and was himself a highly cultured man with an interest in literature and history. Unfortunately he was also the father of at least four illegitimate children and used his position, as well as the wealth that came with it, to advance his own family interests. After failing to mediate a truce between the English and French before the battle of Poitiers, de Heredia fought in the French ranks, was captured and was threatened with execution by the infuriated Black Prince who commanded the English army. Instead de Heredia ransomed himself for 10,000 francs. He was also responsible for organizing the fortification of the papal city of Avignon, where the popes exiled themselves for many years, and did almost more than anyone else to make Avignon the cultural capital of Europe in the late 14th century. As the Pope's favourite, Juan Fernandez de Heredia was imposed upon the Hospitallers as their new Master in 1377.

De Heredia might have been unscrupulous and ambitious but the Prior of Portugal was said to be even worse. He was Father Alvaro Gonçalves Pereira, a man famous for his grandiosity and his disobedience of orders as well as for his personal immorality. In contrast there was Father Inigo d'Alfaro, the captain or commander of the heroic Hospitaller garrison at Izmir in 1403 who also held the rank of Lieutenant to the Drapier. Inigo had earlier commanded the Hospitaller island of Lango and would later defend the Aragonese castle of Alcañiz in 1411.

Slavs rarely rose high in the Hospitaller Order even during these later centuries, but in 1315 a member of the local Silesian elite in what is now Poland, Father Michael, who was possibly from the Tinz family, was recorded as the Master's Lieutenant in this part of Europe. Demoted when his patron, the Master Foulques de Villaret, was forced to resign, Father Michael won the support of the local nobility and in 1317 became Prior of Bohemia, Moravia, Polonia and Austria. This was the first time in almost 80 years that a native of the area had held such a post.

Up to the 1330s most of the leading figures in the neighbouring Priory of Hungary had come from Tuscany in Italy, a large number being from the di Gragnana family. Of course Italians also held positions within Italy, Father Leonardo de Tibertis from the Spoleto area being Prior of Venice from 1312 to 1330 as well as being the Order's Procurator or senior legal and financial official in the papal *curia* or court. Having been recognized as an outstanding administrator, Father Leonardo was sent to England to sort out the Order's severe financial problems there. Indeed he was so successful that the English brethren elected him as their prior and Father Leonardo returned to England to take up this position after leaving Venice in 1330.

In 1467 Giovanni Battista Orsini became the first Italian Master of the Order since the 12th century. Other senior Italian brethren played a significant cultural role in the Italian Renaissance. One such was Father Ludovico Marcello, a doctor of canon law who became Prior of Treviso near Venice. Though Ludovico lived there in luxury and had three illegitimate children, his career also had a more positive aspect as a patron of culture, supporting artists and literary scholars. He also restored the church of San Giovanni and built a new hospital before his death in 1528.

MILITARY TRAINING

Little is known about military training within the Military Orders, despite the fact that young novices must have entered with very limited skill. Their training seems to have been informal and took about a year. It was based upon practical texts in French rather than translations of archaic and theoretical Latin texts. Even after the novitiate system was generally abandoned and replaced by a minimum age of entry, there continued to be a probationary period in the Middle East itself.

Most Hospitaller brothers-in-arms were trained soldiers before they joined the Order. It was popularly said in 12th-century Western Europe that 'You can make a horseman of a lad at puberty, but after that never. He who stays at school until the age of twelve is fit only to be a priest.'

Hospitaller ambassadors in discussion with the Ottoman Sultan. Kneeling between them is the interpreter, a vital role which was normally taken by a Greek. (Obsidionis Rhodie Urbis Descriptio by William Caoursin, f.93r, MS. Lat. 6067, Bibliothèque Nationale de France, Paris)

The undercroft of the central
donjon or main tower of the
Hospitaller castle of Castel
Rouge, Qala'at Ahmar, in Syria.
Guidebooks often describe these
spaces as dungeons, though in
reality their primary purpose
was the storage of food,
weaponry and other vital
supplies. (David Nicolle)

The undercroft of the central
donjon or main tower of the
Hospitaller castle of Castel
Rouge, Qala'at Ahmar, in Syria.
Guidebooks often describe these
spaces as dungeons, though in
reality their primary purpose
was the storage of food,
weaponry and other vital
supplies. (David Nicolle)

From the age of 12 onwards the education of the *jeunes* or 'young warriors
under training', like that of any knight-to-be, focussed on specific military skills
such as riding, discipline, the use of the lance and shield, and the ability to evade
enemy blows. The training of the jeunes was done as a group, which had the
advantage of developing strong comradeship amongst young men who might also
be dubbed knights at the same time. Hugh de Cluny, who became bishop of Le
Mans, recalled how his father, an early 11th-century warrior, had been trained 'to
ride as a young man, to make his horse turn, to shake a spear, use a round shield
and, most abhorrent of all, to despoil and ravage.' Cavalry training was more
complex by the 12th century, but tournaments and jousting soon ceased to be a

The Romano-Byzantine and early Islamic cistern at Bayt Ras which was one of the Hospitallers' most valuable estates in northern Jordan before the entire area was lost to Saladin after the battle of Hattin in 1187. (David Nicolle)

genuine form of military exercise and degenerated into a mere sport. Perhaps for this reason Hospitaller regulations only permitted limited practice jousts in the presence of the Master. Hunting anything other than lions, which were a serious hazard in the Middle East, was also banned, although this prohibition relaxed a little in the 13th century when unauthorized hunting was regarded only as a minor offence. Crossbows could only be used against targets – in other words in military training – but there are plenty of references to crusader knights using crossbows while fighting on foot, and this must also have been true of the Hospitallers.

The couched lance, firmly tucked beneath a cavalryman's arm and used in a close-packed *conrois* of horsemen, demanded considerable riding skill, discipline and unit cohesion. It also entailed the proper use of a shield, as the popular mid-12th-century *Song of Roland* stated: 'Shields on their necks and with their lances well ordered'. There is considerable debate about where this couched technique was first developed, but it was almost certainly not in 11th-century Western Europe, since it had been known in Byzantium and the Islamic world centuries earlier. Its effectiveness was such that it not only added weight and penetration to a thrust but enabled a successful cavalryman to topple a foe from his saddle or even overthrow both man and horse. As the *Song of Roland* again so eloquently put it, 'The girths are burst, the saddles swivel round'.

The *Song of Roland* similarly described young trainees *escrimissent*, fencing or skirmishing, on foot with sword or spear. The little evidence that survives from the medieval period indicates that swordsmanship was firmly associated with the use of the shield. It is likely that later medieval but pre-Renaissance fencing

techniques were a continuation of a long tradition of fighting in full armour. Medieval combat manuals certainly do not contradict the available literary and pictorial evidence of the 12th to 14th centuries, and they also have interesting parallels with training manuals from more literate early and high medieval Byzantine and Islamic civilizations. Compared with the subsequent Renaissance period, medieval fencing used heavier, broader blades. It also had to deal with a greater variety of protective helmets and armour as well as of opposing weapons. Thrusts were usually at the opponent's face while cuts were directed against his legs and feet. Defensive parries used both the sword and the shield.

European combat training manuals from the late 13th and 14th centuries tend to be brutally realistic rather than describing a gentlemanly form of duelling. Where swords are concerned they indicate that the thrust was more effective than the cut, but was more dangerous in 'friendly' combats. In addition to swords, these manuals dealt with other weapons and also with wrestling. Their origins are unknown, but they must surely reflect precisely the sort of skills expected of a fully trained Hospitaller brother-in-arms.

The 14th to 16th centuries were also a period in which much was written on military theory. This was primarily intended for leaders rather than ordinary knights but by the 15th century it covered most aspects of contemporary warfare including archery, siege artillery and firearms. There was by now a 'gentlemanly' manner of fighting that relied upon sophisticated skills rather than brute force. A knight was expected to display skill with weapons and armour, as well as to be agile, to be capable of striking, parrying and evading blows and swift in his reactions. The acquisition of such abilities involved hard training, sometimes with especially heavy weapons. Furthermore, the importance of mental attitudes, the ability to remain calm and to be psychologically prepared for combat were recognized, along with the need to pace oneself and not wear excessively heavy and thus tiring armour. The climate of the Aegean and the chaotic conditions of close combat aboard a warship, in addition to the known danger of getting out of breath when a helmet visor was closed, may account for a widespread preference for open-faced helmets such as *bascinets* and *salets* amongst the Hospitallers.

The use of large amounts of plate armour declined in the later 15th and 16th centuries, largely as a result of the increasing use of firearms. Before that happened, however, the late medieval swordsman faced a great variety of remarkably effective body armour, not always of plate. The initial result was the development of heavier and more pointed sword-blades from the late 13th century onwards. Greater emphasis was given to the *foyne* or thrust though the cut was not neglected. For example, a unique but anonymous late 13th-century Latin text on fencing, written in Germany, shows many complex actions; many thrusts, cuts to shins and feet, as well as sword parries and counter-strikes with a small shield.

OPPOSITE
The Hospitaller Grand Master Pierre d'Aubusson supervising the strengthening of the fortifications of Rhodes city prior to the Ottoman siege of 1480. Written records show that a large proportion of the craftsmen were local Rhodian Greeks. (Obsidionis Rhodie Urbis Descriptio by William Caoursin, f.9v, MS. Lat. 6067, Bibliothèque Nationale, Paris, France; akg-images/Visioars)

Johannes Liechtenauer, the father of German fencing, wrote his *Fechtbuch* or 'Fighting Book' around 1389 and although it has no specific links to the Hospitallers it was compiled by a priest named Hanko Doebringer, a student of Liechtenauer. The first known treatise dealing with a new Italian style of fencing, which relied upon a longsword without a shield, was the *Flos Duellatorium* by Fiore dei Liberi written in 1410. Though he acknowledged the German master's influence, his book dealt with unarmoured combat using a variety of weapons. Other 15th-century Italian and German works described the use of infantry weapons including the pole-axe and two-handed or hand-and-a-half sword. There was even a book on wrestling by one Otto the Jew. Another style of combat which was very widespread during the 15th and early 16th century combined the use of sword and dagger. This was unlikely to have been common while wearing armour or in battle, though it might have been useful aboard ship.

CONVENT LIFE

The conventual life of the Hospitallers was governed by their Rule compiled by the second Master, Raymond du Puy, and was based upon the monastic rule of St Augustine. It revolved around regular religious observances, poverty, chastity, obedience, and communal eating and sleeping. The disruption caused to this lifestyle by warfare and campaigning should not be exaggerated, since fighting was never continuous and only a small number of men were involved at any one time. This was particularly true of those brothers who lived in Western Europe.

Their daily routine was based upon the monastic *horarium* or 'hours', all brothers attending religious services though only a few took an active part in them. Many brothers were illiterate and so were expected merely to listen and say a certain number of *paternosters* (the Lord's Prayer in Latin) for each period of the religious day, to a total of 150 each day. Those brothers away on business or at war were similarly expected to say a certain number of paternosters. Each brother of the Order had to attend Holy Communion at least three times a year a Christmas, Easter and Pentecost. Prayer for the sick were recited every evening by Hospitaller priests, though in convents which lacked their own brother-chaplains, priests from outside the Order were employed.

In convents the brothers went to bed after the service of Compline and rose for the service of Matins. They slep

Part of a stone gaming board found in Belvoir castle. Gambling would have been prohibited amongst Hospitaller brethren, but of course brethren of the Order formed a tiny minority in all such Hospitaller castles. So perhaps this game, whose rules have long been forgotten, was played by servants or mercenaries employed by the Order. (Israel Antiquities Authority)

At the far end of what is believed to have been one of the main dining halls in the Hospitaller castle of Crac des Chevaliers is a row of latrines. These were flushed by a water channel and would probably have had at least a curtain if not a door across the entrance to each cubicle. (David Nicolle)

in wool or linen garments and had to be silent in the dormitories. They were forbidden to sleep naked despite the Middle Eastern heat, nor might they share beds in the cold of winter, and a candle was always burning in the dormitory. In the smaller houses in Europe, and in the granges or isolated farms owned by the Order, the regulation about not sleeping alone could not always be followed. Even as early as the 1170s the rule was also relaxed for senior men such as the Master, who acquired their own private rooms or cells, and by the end of the 13th century even some ordinary brothers enjoyed comparable privacy. The Master continued to live next to the headquarters, although the Marshal and the other brothers' dormitories had moved away. By 1265 the Marshal lived in the auberge in Acre, as did the conventual baillis and ex-baillis by 1288.

Eating was supposedly also done communally, though during the 13th century some men obtained the right to eat alone in their cells. According to a statute of 1268 the Master Sergeant and Master Crossbowman could not eat at the same table at the brothers because, despite their titles, they were not brothers of the Order. The physician and surgeon could, however, eat with the brothers. Most monks were prohibited from eating the meat of four-footed animals and at first this applied to the Hospitallers as well, but the rule was gradually relaxed. This was particularly the case when brothers were on campaign and needed to keep up their strength, and eventually such meat was only banned on Fridays. There was a similar increase in the allowance of extra food and drink known as *pittances* under certain circumstances. The fasts which the Hospitallers had to observe were less than those endured by ordinary monks, again for military reasons, and

The Hospitaller estate of Kolossi in Cyprus included a very valuable sugar-making factory as well as a simple castle. The exportation of sugar from the Middle East to Western Europe was an important source of income for the Hospitallers. (akg-images/ Bildarchiv Steffens)

most were in winter rather than in the campaigning season of summer. In fact, there were efforts to stop over-enthusiastic brothers fasting excessively because this could undermine their military effectiveness. Even the rule against talking while eating was more lenient than that of other monastic orders. Nor was it always obeyed and there were complaints of rowdy brothers beating the servants who brought the food or even pelting them with pieces of bread.

In the eyes of the outside world, the brothers of the Hospitallers appeared to eat well. They were summoned to the refectory by a bell twice a day and the

food was brought by paid servants. Each meal usually had two sittings, the second for those on duty during the first, and for those fasting. In 1206 the first meal was before the religious service of Nones, the second after the service of Vespers and no wine was drunk after Compline. In practice, the staple diet seems to have been cooked meats, fish, eggs, bread and wine. All brothers ate the same quality food and this had to be good enough to be 'stomached', or not cause indigestion. It was certainly not ascetic fare, though in periods of abstinence the brothers gave up meat. In Lent the brethren drank no milk and there were neither eggs nor cheese on Fridays. The rules were also relaxed while at sea and additional pittances, especially of wine, became more common during the 13th century, particularly for those who bled themselves for medicinal reasons. After a meal the brethren rose and went in procession to say grace in their church.

HOSPITALLER DISCIPLINE

Justice and discipline within the Order were based upon its Rule and Statutes, and remained a constant feature of Hospitaller administration as well as the daily life of brethren. Further usances or customs grew up over the years, resulting in an often confusing, complex and uncertain system of justice. Some things were, however, clear. For example, accusations concerning breaches of the rules could

Temple Cressing in England was another valuable ex-Templar property which was transferred to the Hospitallers early in the 14th century. The village still has the 13th-century barn which is so large that it has been suggested that the commandery of Cressing served as a depot where the produce of several such estates could be stored before being shipped down the nearby river Brain and thence by coastal craft to London. (B. Hillman-Crouch)

only be made before the Chapter. A brother who complained publicly of another before chastising him in private, or who denounced him outside the Chapter but in front of other brothers, would suffer the same penalty as that of the accused if the 'slandered' brother brought a complaint. The system of justice and complaints involved the most senior men and their actions, none being above the law, but once a brother decided to make a complaint, the system was formal and solemn. The earliest recorded such *esgart* dated from around 1170. There were, in practice, three parts of an esgart: a formal plaint, the hearing of evidence, and the judgement of the Chapter. A fourth part may have involved an appeal to higher authority. The accused and the accuser could call witnesses and these were interrogated in the presence of both parties. While the procedure was very formal, the punishments were carefully scaled and similar to those in other religious orders. They ranged from the convicted being denied wine or cooked food or both, up to a permanent 'loss of habit', meaning expulsion from the Order. Denial of cooked food or wine was the only punishment that could be imposed by a community of brethren without recourse to judgement by the Chapter. In Syria this punishment was imposed for misbehaviour at meals, laziness or being disorderly in the auberge.

Hospitaller life was neither ascetic nor scholarly but it was disciplined. Rules on what could be termed military behaviour ranged from the specific to the general. For example a brother was not allowed to gallop his horse, unless ordered

This massive storage chamber is in Marqab, or Margat, castle which was one of the Order of Hospitallers' most important fortresses on the coast of Syria. It could hold enough supplies for the garrison to endure a very long siege. (David Nicolle)

to do so by the bailli, but was permitted to canter. The Rule of the Templars forbade military service in the armies of Muslim Turkish Seljuks of Anatolia, but the Hospitallers' Rule made no mention of this matter. In 1238 Pope Gregory IX wrote a letter to the Hospitallers in Acre during the preparations for crusades, stating that he had heard that brothers kept harlots in their villages, owned private property, and in some cases were suspected of heresy. He gave the brethren three months to reform themselves or he would send the Archbishop of Tyre to reform them. No evidence survives of such crimes but the rumour may have been based upon a Chapter meeting, after which the matter was hushed up.

Punishments for breaches of the rules usually consisted of religious penances, though 'loss of habit' was the penalty for fornication. For striking a fellow brother it was the *quarantaine*, meaning 40 days' expulsion and temporary loss of habit. A lesser penalty was *septaine*, or seven days' similar punishment. Clearly, Rhodes was not free from tensions between the brethren, and the worst case of internal violence came in 1381 when a Gascon Hospitaller, Father Bertrin de Gagnac, was suspected of involvement in the drowning of the Drapier who was the most senior Spanish brother on the island. Gagnac was a successful, influential and rich brother but he in turn now accused a senior Rhodian citizen of spreading malicious rumours. This resulted in a trial during which several women were tortured to confess that they had indeed spread rumours.

No evidence was found but Bertrin de Gagnac was nevertheless suspected of embezzling money and soon faced direct accusations. This resulted in a trial in 1381, as a result of which he was deprived of his habit but, as the Master tried to remove the cloak, de Gagnac struck him with a dagger. The Master was only slightly wounded while de Gagnac was cut down by the Master's guards. A year later, 56 brethren and donati, 51 of whom were French, were sent back to their European priories, supposedly because the Order could not afford to maintain them in Rhodes. In reality this was probably a disciplinary measure reflecting tensions between French, Spaniards and others. Nor is it clear that all of them actually left the island.

Dressing and Arming the Brethren

CLOTHING

OPPOSITE

Joseph Chauncy, the Hospitaller Prior of England around 1273, in prayer before John the Baptist. The latter, however, also carries the symbol of the Apostle John, a lamb and flag.(Missal of Joseph Chauncy, private collection)

The wearing of colourful, expensive clothes and the use of decorated military equipment and horse-harness was very much part of the medieval knight's way of life. When a man entered one of the Military Orders all this changed, though it proved difficult to ensure that all the dress, harness or equipment regulations were followed. Hospitaller statutes constantly prohibited this or that form of decorated equipment and eventually the regulations were relaxed. Yet the basic Rule was never changed. Some of these statutes shed an interesting light on how individual Hospitaller brothers behaved. For example, a statute of the Master Hugh Revel in 1262 stated that the wearing of *espaliers d'armes* (mail or padded shoulder defences) or *chausses* (leg protectors, presumably the armoured form made of mail) was forbidden at certain times such as prayers. The fact that this statute had to be repeated in a late 13th-century esgart suggests that the practice had continued. Perhaps Master Nicholas de Lorgne's statute, dated 4 August 1278 at Acre, insisting that no armour be worn within the precincts of the Hospitaller House during the elections of a new Master, hinted at earlier attempts at intimidation by armed men.

No Hospitaller brother-in-arms was allowed more than the regulation amount of military equipment, unless he was given special permission. This meant that the Military Orders appeared more standardized than ordinary secular knights. It may also have reflected the limited amount of kit available. Shortages would similarly have accounted for the effort the Hospitallers put into the recycling of arms, armour, horse-harness and even clothing. None of these items belonged to the brother who used it and consequently all reverted to the Order on his death. The Master, Grand Commander, Marshal, Hospitaller in charge of the infirmary and his subordinate the Infirmarian, the Drapier, Treasurer and Conventual Prior

The early 12th-century relief carvings of knights and foot soldiers in Pavia cathedral show that there were still many similarities between medieval Italian military equipment and that of the Islamic side of the Mediterranean. For example, the infantryman seen here carries a tall but flat-based mantlet shield of a kind also used in 12th-century Egypt, Syria and perhaps even further afield. (in situ, Pavia cathedral; Pavia cathedral photograph)

all had claims upon such matériel. This could lead to confusion if not argument, so the whole issue was carefully regulated. The Master received the keys of all deceased baillis, the Marshal received the keys of deceased brethren-in-arms (both knights and sergeants), the Grand Commander those of brethren-in-office. Even so, there could be disputes because some men held multiple or temporary offices. The Master Esquire, the brother-of-the-parmentarie and the Infirmarian, who were themselves the subordinates of the Marshal, Drapier and Hospitaller respectively, jointly put the deceased's belongings in a sealed sack that could only be reopened in their presence.

Mid-13th-century Hospitaller usances show that the objects were divided into distinct sections. Horses and related equipment went to the Marshal, as did arms and armour, while bedding went to the Drapier, as did most clothing and unused cloth. Table and kitchen items, books, liturgical and other miscellaneous items from capitular baillis and from the Master's own companions went to the Master. Those of other brethren-at-arms went to the Marshal, but those of regular baillis, 'local commanders' and all brethren-in-office went to the Grand Commander. No specific mention was made of money but this probably went to the Treasury.

According to a statute of 1288 all armour also escheated, or in other words was handed back, when a brother left the Middle East. It was placed in the keeping of a brother appointed by the Marshal. Such equipment then became available to other brethren-in-arms who might want to make an exchange for what they already had. Crossbows were a special case, since these had to be placed in the Treasury before returning to the Arbalestry. Some later usances were more detailed, for example specifying that Turkish carpets, saddles, javelins, *bardings* (horse coverings), *gonfalons* (flags), *pennoncelles* (small pennons), chargers (war horses), hacks (riding horses), mules, Turkish weapons, axes, all forms of armour and harness for animals, *arcs de bodoc* (pellet bows), table knives, crossbows, all forms of armour for men, swords, lances, *coreaus de fetur* (leather cuirasses), *playines* (plate armour), mail hauberks, *gipelles* (quilted soft armours), *soubre seignals* (perhaps surcoats), *chapels de fers* (brimmed helmets) and bascinets (close-fitting helmets) of dead brothers went to the Marshal.

The habit of the Hospitallers was a genuine uniform, though in the early decades it was more suited to the life of a monk than a fighting man.

Another early 12th-century carved panel in Pavia cathedral illustrates armoured cavalrymen, one of whom seems to be checking his horse's saddle or girth. (in situ, Pavia cathedral; Pavia cathedral photograph)

Close inspection of this early 12th-century carved capital shows that the body armour worn by St George seems to consist of two different elements. They are a normal long-sleeved mail hauberk with an integral coif beneath the helmet, plus an apparent lamellar cuirass around the middle of the saint's body. (in situ, cathedral, Aulnay; CESCM, Poitiers, France)

The standard black *cappae* were relatively tight-fitting monastic robes and these the brothers-in-arms had to wear over their armour even on campaign. It was clearly not suited to the violent movement of close combat, yet it was not until 1248 that Pope Innocent IV accepted the Hospitallers' complaints and allowed brethren-in-arms to 'wear wide surcoats, bearing upon the breast the sign of the Cross', but only in 'dangerous areas'. Coloured cloth, velvet and the expensive luxury skins of wild animals were prohibited. Crosses were sewn or embroidered on the breasts of the cappae and mantles, though these could apparently be removed when travelling in non-Christian countries. The Armenians knew the Hospitallers as 'Brethren who wear garments marked with the sign of the Cross'.

In the late 13th and early 14th centuries the brethren's mantle folded entirely around the body, was made of black or dark brown cloth and opened in the front where it could also be closed with buttons of the same cloth. In Europe the mantle was worn fully closed. On the front of this mantle was a cross, 7 to 10 cm wide and now in the characteristic eight-pointed form first seen in the early 13th century. The 'conventual shoes' worn on most occasions are not really understood but were presumably very simple. After 1300 such shoes were still worn by servants of the Order but no longer by full Hospitaller brethren.

Throughout this period the Hospitallers remained visibly distinctive and although modesty was the primary objective of their costume regulations, they often appeared well dressed to ordinary people. Certainly the normal issue of clothing recorded in 1206 seemed abundant by the standards of the day. It consisted of three shirts, three pairs of breeches, one *cotta* or tunic, one *cappa* coif or hood, one *garnache* coat and hood, two mantles or cloaks, one of which was lined with simple non-luxury fur, one pair of hose of linen and one of wool, three bed-sheets and a sack in which to keep them. The reforms of 1295 mentioned a yearly issue of two suits consisting of a cotta and undertunic, garnache and mantle, one of which was again lined with simple fur. These, however, included the livery or heavier ceremonial robes and the robes of pittance, which were made of thin cloth for use in summer. By 1283 it had become customary to wear a livery robe in winter and a robe of pittance in summer. The livery robe could be taken out of store if needed in summer or could be worn throughout the year, but this was not the case with the robe of pittance.

Five years later brothers were allowed to wear black or dark brown mantles which folded entirely around the body and incorporated a *gorgiere* or large collar. *Hargans* (long coats) and *cotes hardies* (short coats) were initially forbidden, although hargans became acceptable by 1300 when the cross of the Order had to be sewn on them as well as on the cappae and mantles. The garnache had now to be open in the front with seven buttons of the same cloth. Cotes hardies with points (laces to which the hose and other garments could be attached) were, however, still not acceptable. A further decree of 1305 stated that the mantle, cappa, *rondel* (probably a type of scarf) and hargan must all be black.

On his head a brother wore a white coif. At first this had to be of double thickness, though later it was allowed to be worn 'simple', which probably means of single thickness. Only during certain church services could the coif be worn on its own. Otherwise it was covered by a large skull cap which had to touch the wearer's ears on both sides. This cap was removed only for Gospel readings, during the most sacred moment of the Mass, out of respect for a superior or for other 'reasonable causes'. In the 1280s a usance drawn up by the Commander in Cyprus repeated that a brother must not remove his *biretta* or hat even if he was feeling hot, unless there was a good reason. A brother could also wear a brimmed hat, a white turban or *oreillet* (item covering the ears) in the fierce Middle Eastern sun. Many Westerners had adopted Arab head-cloths as a sensible protection during the Syrian summer and in 1262 the Hospitaller Master Hugh Revel accepted a statute that stated that no brother on a military expedition could wear a turban that was anything other than white, which was embroidered or which dangled down to his waist. The prohibition against embroidered or non-white turbans had to be repeated in Cyprus in 1295 when it was also stated that only white oreillets that fully covered the ears might be worn.

In the first Hospitaller Rule, brothers were not allowed *planeaus* (sandals) or *galoches* (large overshoes worn in the Islamic world) but only *soliers* or ordinary shoes. From the late 12th century a Hospitaller brother was, however, permitted boots during night-time and a complex set of regulations then developed which allowed him to keep his boots on at certain other times. A reaction may have set in at Acre in 1270, when a statute of Master Hugh Revel stated that 'Concerning estiveaus [boots], all are forbidden (except when armed) as soon as he shall disarm himself, that he put them off or that he put over them his soliers [shoes].' These boots may have been of the loose, soft leather Middle Eastern variety which had been adopted by many European settlers in the Crusader States. The problem of footwear persisted and in late 13th-century Cyprus pointed boots and *chausses avantpiés* (hose incorporating a pointed shoe) were entirely prohibited.

The cost of such clothing was high and seems to have accounted for a surprising proportion of the Order's finances. In 1219 the cost of a robe for one new brother was 40 shillings when this was paid by King Henry III of England. From the mid-13th century, brothers were increasingly given permission to buy their own clothes, and were issued a set amount of money to do so. Each brother was also given a small amount of pocket-money, which the vain were said to have wasted on clothes of a more fashionable cut or better cloth, embroidered

The armoured guardsman standing behind the ruler in this manuscript made in Acre in the late 13th century serves as a good representation of the military equipment and costume used during the final years of the Crusader States. He is also of interest because of the distinctive basilard style of dagger on his hip, this being amongst the earliest illustrations of such a weapon. (Story of Troy, f.89v, MS. 562, Bibliothèque Municipale, Dijon, France)

kerchiefs or turbans, brighter colours, silk, silver or gold thread, and even jewellery. Frequent decrees by the main Chapter of the Order tried to stop this practice but apparently had little effect.

In 1259 Pope Alexander IV granted distinctive costume to the brother-knights of the Hospitallers, there previously having been no difference between the dress of knights and sergeants. Other comparable institutions including the Templars already employed such distinctions and so now 'The knights who are brethren in your Order shall wear black mantles in order that they may be distinguished from the other brethren of the said Order [who presumably wore dark brown]. In war, however, and in battle they shall wear jupons and other military surcoats which shall be of a red colour, having sewn upon them a white cross exactly as upon your standard.' The new rule was revoked after 19 years, perhaps having had a bad effect on morale, and all brethren-in-arms soon wore a scarlet *jupon* or *jupell* in battle.

CLOTHING IN THE 14TH AND 15TH CENTURIES

The 14th and 15th centuries were a period of fundamental change in Western European male costume, with a move away from the loose clothes that had much in common with the Greek Orthodox, Eastern European and Middle Eastern attire. Instead the distinctively Western fashion for tight-fitting, almost body-hugging,

OPPOSITE PAGE
One of the most extraordinary objects excavated along with many other important pieces of 13th- or early 14th-century Mamluk military equipment in the Citadel of Damascus is half a helmet made of wood, cloth and perhaps leather. It is so different in shape, structure and external decoration from other wood-lined 'hard hats' found at the same time that it may actually have been captured from the crusaders. (Syrian National Museum Conservation Department, Damascus; David Nicolle)

male fashions saw its birth during these centuries. The Hospitallers, whose traditional garments reflected the Order's religious origins, were not immune from such changes. Indeed, many pictorial sources show that the brethren, when not actually involved in religious duties, wore clothes that differed little from those of the secular knightly class. This was obviously true during their military duties, whether or not they were wearing armour. These new and distinctive Western European fashions also helped the Hospitallers, like other Latins in the eastern Mediterranean and Aegean regions, to make a visual distinction between themselves and Greek Orthodox Christians – even more so between themselves and Muslims.

Meanwhile, even the Hospitallers' peacetime black mantle with its eight-pointed white cross diverged into several different garments, ranging from a traditional full-length cloak with or without a hood, to a short tabard-like garment that did not even reach the knees. The old prohibition against decorated weapons and other such 'splendour' had been virtually abandoned, and there are frequent references to red sword-belts and swords with silvered if not gilded decorations. Pictorial sources again illustrate sometimes magnificent decoration such as gilded fringed surcoats, sumptuous embroidery and etched or engraved armour. Somehow Master Jean Parisot de la Valette's ruling in 1558 that knights caught wearing embroidered stockings could face four years in the galleys does not sound entirely convincing as proof that Hospitaller brethren spurned worldly magnificence.

This effigy of a French nobleman, Jean d'Alluye, who died in 1248, came from the abbey of Clarte-Dieu. It has attracted attention because its sword is unlike anything else seen in Europe at this time. It has even been suggested that it represents a Chinese sword, brought westward by the invading Mongols, which then came into Jean d'Alluye's hands and remained one of his most prized possessions. (Cloisters Museum, New York, USA; David Nicolle)

ARMOUR AND ARMS IN THE 12TH AND 13TH CENTURIES

The *guarnement* or arms and armour used by Hospitaller brethren-in-arms was the same as that of other knights and sergeants, except for its general lack of decoration. During the 12th century the guarnement remained relatively basic and usually consisted of some or all the following items: shield, surcoat, sword, sometimes a *coutel* or dagger, *afeutreüre*, which may have been an early form of felt padding or soft-armour worn beneath the hauberk, the mail hauberk itself, quilted chausses for the legs, sometimes mail chausses for the most heavily armoured men, a helmet, and a long cavalry lance or shorter infantry spear with leather binding around its grip. The mace was still regarded as an Islamic weapon, or one used by non-noble infantry.

Descriptions of men arming themselves are found in secular literature of the period, but not in Hospitaller documents. The mid- to late 12th-century *Romance of Aucassin and Nicolette*, for example, states that the hero dressed in a double hauberk. The man then laced his helmet to his head, grasped his sword, mounted his warhorse and took his shield and lance, finally glancing down at his feet to ensure that his spurs were correct.

Even more detailed is a description of what was needed by a knight according to Arnaut Guilhem de Marsan in the 1170s:

> Have a good warhorse, and I will tell you what kind. One that is swift running and apt for arms. Take this one at once, and then your armour, lance and sword and hauberk… Let the horse be well tested and not a poor one, and put on it a good saddle and bridle and a really fine breast-strap so that nothing is unsuitable… Have a pack-horse to carry your doubled hauberk, and your weapons held high so that they appear more attractive, and always have the squires close by you.

The composition of a 'doubled hauberk' is still a matter of dispute amongst armour historians. It clearly did not mean that the mail links were joined together in a different manner but might have indicated that two hauberks were worn, one perhaps having short sleeves and a shorter hem. Another interpretation might refer to the hauberk plus the padding which must always have been necessary beneath it. Certainly the quilted *aketon*, *gambais* and *gambeson* were used in this way in the 13th century, by which time the wearing of an old gambeson, or one blackened by the mail hauberk above, was considered a sign of poverty. In the Middle East, however, knights including members of the Military Orders sometimes wore quilted armour without the heavier mail hauberk, particularly in summer, when scouting or while harassing an enemy as light cavalry.

There is little evidence of military equipment, at least that of iron, being made in the Crusader States. Some would have been captured from the Muslims but the great bulk of arms and armour used by the Hospitallers was imported from Europe. Armour was also expensive and took a long time to manufacture. It has been estimated that a complete sword took at least 200 man-hours, a full mail hauberk weighing some 25 kilograms (55 pounds) taking several weeks. Information from late 12th- to mid-13th-century Genoa, which was a centre of the arms trade, shows that a full mail hauberk was approximately five times as expensive as a separate mail coif, a cuirass and a *panceriam* (lighter mail armour) being less than half that of a hauberk. Comparable information from Venice in the 1220s indicates that a helmet cost 30 denarii, a sword from 45 to 50, a knife or dagger 20. Even a crossbow quarrel or arrow cost one denarius. To compare the value of various types of money at different times is difficult and potentially misleading. Nevertheless, it is worth noting that in 1262 it cost 2,000 silver deniers of Tours fully to equip a Hospitaller knight, which was expensive, and in 1303 it cost 1,500 deniers to equip a sergeant.

Acre was a major centre of trade to and from the neighbouring Islamic countries; leather boots, shoes, horse-harness, saddles and unworked leather were imported from the Muslim world along with bows, arrows and horses. But the little information that does refer to arms manufacture in the Crusader States indicates that non-metallic objects such as shields were made in Jerusalem, and crossbows in Acre. The iron elements of crossbows were being sent from Genoa to the Crusader States in the early 13th century, which suggests that once again local crusader craftsmen only dealt with wood, horn, sinew, leather and such organic material.

A chronic shortage of military equipment in the Crusader States is similarly indicated by the Hospitallers' overriding concern that weaponry only move in one direction; namely from West to East. Even the lending of military equipment by one brother to another required special permission. Brothers travelling from Europe to the Middle East were expected to bring full military kit with them while brothers going back to Europe were issued with the bare minimum. Senior men, such as newly appointed baillis travelling to the Middle East, normally brought what was described as a *passage* of armour, even sending this on its own if they themselves were unable to make the journey. In 1293 the Master Jean de Villiers, based in Cyprus since the fall of Acre, issued a ruling that brothers returning from the West must not only bring full harness (armour) with them, but also three 'beasts' – horses or perhaps pack-animals. The question of equipment was so urgent that when an envoy from the Prior of Castile died in Cyprus in 1303 there was a heated legal argument about whether his armour should remain in the East or should be returned to Spain. It had been purchased by the prior specifically for this journey and was to be returned afterwards; nevertheless it was eventually handed over to the Marshal in Cyprus.

The Castellaria or 'Commercial Exchange Centre', overlooking a square just inside the main harbour or Marine Gate of Rhodes, was intended to be one of the most important buildings in the city. However, it was completed in 1507, only 15 years before the Hospitaller-ruled island finally fell to the Ottoman Turks. (Hervé Champollion/akg-images)

As far as the weapons of a brother-in-arms were concerned, the cavalry lance remained the most important. This was normally about three metres (10ft) long with a shaft often, perhaps usually, of spruce. Flags and pennons appear to have been nailed to the shafts rather than being laced or tied on. An object called a *hantier* appears in some early 13th-century sources and this may have been a form of support for the butt of the lance while it was being carried vertically.

The sword was the most prestigious weapon, though it was of secondary importance in a cavalry charge. Most surviving examples weigh from 1 to 1½ kilograms (2–3 pounds). Those garnished with silver were specifically banned in Hospitaller houses, though the application of tin, silver and even gold to the *quillons* (the crossguard of a sword) and pommel of swords was not merely decorative as it also protected them from rust. The sword *baldric*, a strap to carry the scabbard suspended from the right shoulder, had largely gone out of fashion by the mid-12th century, to be replaced by a sword-belt that was secured at the front by slit and knotted thongs rather than a buckle. The buckled sword-belt appeared in the later 13th century. Meanwhile, various methods of tying the split thong ends of the two parts of the belt to the scabbard were used. This complex system was eventually replaced by metallic rings on the sides of the scabbard itself, an Asian or Middle Eastern system that had fallen out of use in Western Europe following the collapse of the Roman Empire.

Daggers had been widely used in the Islamic world but in 12th-century Europe they seem to have been despised by the knightly elite. It may therefore be significant that one of the earliest references to a *misericorde* or coutel dagger in medieval Western literature was in *Les Chétifs*, part of the Old French Crusade

Cycle written in the late 12th century. Such close-combat weapons became much more common in the 13th century. *Les Chétifs* also referred to maces, though these were still associated with Turks or Saracens, as well as Danish axes, *guisarmes d'acier* (long-hafted infantry axes) and *faussars affilés* (infantry weapons with a long blade), all of which were placed in the hands of Christian infantry. The turcopoles in *Les Chétifs* were armed with bows, but it is perhaps significant that many crusaders, including those defending Acre in 1291, used Western European simple bows made of a single stave of wood as well as composite bows of Middle Eastern or Mediterranean form.

Hospitaller statutes stated that brethren-in-arms should tie their armour into a bundle and place it behind their saddle while on campaign, but should always wear helmets and leg armour in hostile territory. They may also have carried a shield. Less detail is known about the armour itself. Primitive or simple forms were clearly used in isolated or poor regions of Europe, but this is unlikely to have been true of the Hospitallers since the organization was not only wealthy but placed great emphasis on the possession of 'suitable' kit. Quite how far oriental influence from the Islamic world upon the armour of regions like Italy and Spain also affected Military Orders and Crusader States is unknown. It seems likely, however, that it would have done so. For example, the characteristic use of hardened leather defences in 13th- and 14th-century Italy may also have been true of Hospitaller garrisons in the Holy Land. The same would have been true of the mail-lined, padded and fabric-covered Islamic *khazaghand*, which was known in Italy as the *ghiazzerino*, in the late 12th-century Crusader States as the *auberc jaserant* and in France as the *jazrain hauberk*.

Medieval mail armour was normally of relatively soft iron with a low carbon content. The wire for the links was drawn, which gave it an internal spiral structure, and alternate links were riveted. References to mail hauberks without coifs in the 12th century do not prove the existence of separate mail coifs. These are normally thought to have appeared in the 13th century, though they were again used much earlier in the Middle East. Practical experiments suggest that the prolonged wearing of mail in hot weather was not a particular problem, but the weight of such garments and their tendency to flap about tired the wearer.

Other less common forms of body armour included the *panceriam* which could have one long sleeve and an integral coif, leather cuirasses which seem more typical of the Iberian peninsula than elsewhere, the French *cuirie* which was probably made of leather to which metallic plates were subsequently added, and the coat-of-plates which first appeared in the second half of the 13th century.

The *manicles de fer* or integral mail mittens at the end of the long sleeves of a mail hauberk were first mentioned, and first appear in art, in the late 12th century. Other more complex forms of protection for the arms had to wait another century or more. Additional protection for the legs developed earlier. In *Les Chétifs*, for example, chausses were described as 'white like the flowers of the meadow', though it is not entirely clear whether this meant mail chausses or padded linen *cuisses*. A slightly later part of the Old French Crusade Cycle, *Elioxe*, which was written in the early 13th century, mentions *genellières*, which are believed to have been early forms of knee defence, 'hanging like window coverings'.

Helmets were kept in place by laces or chin-straps. The straps were specifically described as going over the *ventail* or mail flap which protected the throat, chin and sometimes the lower part of the face. Helmets could be silvered, largely as a protection against rust, but Hospitaller regulations do not specify whether or not this form of apparent decoration was permitted. *Les Chétifs* provided one of the earliest references to a helmet of *quir boli* or hardened leather, though this was worn by a Saracen.

The growing threat from crossbows in Western European warfare, and from composite bows in the Middle East, led to increased protection for a warrior's face. At first this took the form of an ever broader and perhaps longer *nasal* on the helmet, but then complete face-masks or rigid visors were attached to helmets of various shapes. Yet another section of the Old French Crusade Cycle, called *Le Chevalier au Cigne*, which dates from the late 12th or early 13th century, provides a detailed and remarkably early description of a helmet with almost complete facial protection. Its various elements included the *maistre* or bowl, the *candelabres* that may have been a sort of strengthening frame or rim, the *fenestral* which seems to have been part or all of the visor or face-mask, the traditional nasal to which the

The two almost identical effigies found in a now ruined abbey church in north-western England provide some of the earliest and clearest representations of fully enclosed so-called barrel helmets. They date from the second quarter of the 13th century. (Site Museum, Furness Abbey, England; David Nicolle)

OPPOSITE
Some mid-12th-century carvings in northern Spain illustrate a form of helmet which is not seen elsewhere in Europe and may well have been copied from Moorish Andalusian regions further south. It protected more of the face and probably reflected a greater use of archery in Iberian warfare. (in situ, church of Santa Maria la Real, Sanguesa, Spain; David Nicolle)

face-mask might have been attached, the *mentonal* or chin-strap, and *uellière* or eye-slits. This helmet was, however, still worn over a coif with a *ventalle* or ventail. *Elioxe* similarly mentions a helmet with an *uellière*, through which an arrow might penetrate, as well as a *flanboiant* or cloth covering to protect the wearer from the sun. The earliest 13th-century references to the *cervellière* suggest that the term meant the upper part of the skull of a helmet rather than a separate form of head protection. Pictorial evidence shows that the earliest form of separate, small, hemispherical and somewhat close-fitting cervellière helmet was sometimes worn beneath a mail coif. Later this cervellière increased in size with extensions to protect the sides and back of the head, in which case it was worn over a coif.

The coif itself came in a variety of forms, apart from the simple and non-protective cloth type worn as a basic item of dress. In the 11th century the mail coif may have been called a *chapelier* in France but by the late 12th century the term coif was normal. Such protective coifs could also be described as *fort et turcoise* which possibly meant having their own quilted lining. The throat-and-chin-covering ventail developed during the 12th century, though more primitive versions were certainly known earlier. By the late 12th century the term *clavain* had appeared, but it is unclear whether this was regarded as the neck part of the coif or was (more probably) seen as the reinforced neck part of a hauberk which might otherwise lack an integral coif.

European, crusader and thus also Hospitaller shields were almost invariably of wood and were usually covered in leather but their size, shape and probably thickness varied considerably during the 12th and 13th centuries. One of the few

Closer inspection of some of the better-quality military effigies provides information that might otherwise be overlooked. In this mid-13th-century Norman French effigy from Ouville l'Abbaye, for example, the front part of the mail coif is clearly not lined with any other material, but is worn over a 'soft armour' whose vertical quilting can just be seen around the wearer's neck. (Musée Municipale, Rouen, France; David Nicolle)

specialized forms was the very large *talevaz*, sometimes used by men on foot, which might better be called a mantlet since it could probably be rested on the ground.

ARMOUR AND ARMS IN THE 14TH TO 16TH CENTURIES

The 14th and 15th centuries saw greater changes in Western European armour, if not weapons, than any other period. Since the Hospitallers always attempted to have the best and most modern military equipment, their armour was adapted to these developments. For a start, the 14th century saw a shift away from a primary reliance on mail towards an increasing use of plate. Plate body and limb protections of hardened leather and of iron had been known in Europe for a century or so, and their further adoption during the 14th century was not a regular process. Traditional and supposedly more advanced forms of armour coexisted at the same time and sometimes in the same regions. Generally speaking, however, the old-fashioned styles tended to be relegated to less developed, marginal or poorer countries such as Wales, Scotland, Ireland and parts of Scandinavia. Climatic factors also played a part, limiting or slowing the adoption of iron plate armour in hot regions like Italy, Spain, Latin Greece and the Balkans. In all these areas, hardened leather armour became a feature.

The surviving evidence indicates that the arms and armour used in Rhodes and other Hospitaller garrisons were imported from any place able to supply it. In the 14th century, for example, an English nobleman, Henry, Lord Fitzhugh, obtained customs exemption to send a tapestry, 38 sheaves of arrows and 72 bowstrings for use in Bodrum, which surely indicates that English-style longbows were used there.

The remarkable collection of late 15th- and early 16th-century armour found in Rhodes about a hundred years ago, and now scattered across several museums, was made in Italy, Germany, the Iberian

RIGHT

In contrast to the earlier French effigy from Normandy, this German effigy clearly shows that the wearer's mail coif is lined with some form of fabric or perhaps soft leather for additional comfort. It represents Heinrich Otto, the Landgraf of Hessen, and dates from around 1320. (in situ, church of St Elizabeth, Marburg, Germany; David Nicolle)

OPPOSITE

The variety and distinctiveness of 13th- and 14th-century Italian military equipment, and its close technological links with the Islamic world, are epitomized in this effigy of Guido Pallavicino. He is believed to have been a Templar and his effigy dates from around 1301. One of its most remarkable features is the scale or perhaps poorly represented lamellar cuirass that he wears over an otherwise typically European mail hauberk. (in situ, abbey church of San Bernardo, Fontevivo, Italy; Andrea Babuin)

peninsula and other parts of Western Europe. Nevertheless, and for obvious geographical as well as economic or industrial reasons, Italy was the primary source of Hospitaller armour during the 13th and 14th centuries, as it is likely to have been in previous centuries.

References to the use of 'Turkish' military equipment and horse-harness in 13th- and early 14th-century Hospitaller documents indicate that the Order also owned captured matériel. How far this was true during the rest of the 14th and 15th centuries is unknown. However, the references to Turkish equipment suggest the fascinating possibility that the Hospitallers played a role in the transfer of Islamic and Asiatic military technology to Western Europe. It seems clear that Byzantine, and more particularly eastern Islamic or Central Asian styles of armour, including those made using sophisticated leather-working techniques, did influence the development of various forms of armour and helmets in Europe. This was undoubtedly the case with body armour such as the coat-of-plates, brigandine and perhaps also the scale-lined and quilted jack, as well as helmets such as some forms of bascinet.

The armour, some of it far from new, which the Hospitallers abandoned at Rhodes in 1522, mostly consists of what would today be called munitions equipment. In other words it was not the fine and expensive specimens of the armourer's art that normally survived in noble collections and that now fill most armour museums. It was ordinary kit and very few of the individual items are of high quality. This now scattered collection shows what most fighting men really used in the 15th and early 16th centuries, be they Hospitallers or otherwise. Some of the equipment was probably brought to Rhodes by men sent from priories around Europe. Other pieces were probably purchased from armour merchants and reflected what the buyer found most comfortable. In its lack of the uniformity that tends to be characteristic of medieval illustrations of armoured men, the Hospitaller armour tends to destroy modern romantic images of the knight. Instead it consists of an odd mixture of shapes, sizes and styles, some decorated but mostly plain. Much of the armour is also patched and repaired or had been altered during a long and useful life. Very little of it would have appeared shiny or new even when being used.

The recycling of military equipment, which had been characteristic of the Hospitaller Order since the 12th century, continued at least until the 16th century. In 1555, for example, the statutes of the Master Claude de la Sengle repeated that the weapons of deceased brethren should revert to the Order, though with interesting exceptions. Paragraph 24, volume D of his statutes states: 'All arms of whatever description left by Knights deceased, either in Malta or abroad, become the property of the Treasury. They shall be kept in order so as to be available, in case of want, for the protection of our convent [the island]. Exception shall, however, be made in the case of swords and daggers which shall be sold by public auction.'

The Hospitallers were enthusiastic when it came to the adoption of firearms, the Prior of Catalonia having a *bombarda* or heavy cannon as early as 1395. In 1531 the Order in Malta was still eager to obtain good cannon whenever possible and in that year a ship arrived from England laden with guns, a gift from King Henry VIII instead of the 20,000 crowns cash that he had promised to the Master five years earlier. Apparently these gifts ranged from large cannon to small items, including a shield with a handgun in the centre, which still exists.

Several descriptions of the process of arming a knight survive from this period and although none of them relate specifically to a Hospitaller they remain relevant.

Morini may not have been amongst the greatest artists of the later Italian Renaissance but his attention to detail makes him a valuable source of information about the costume and military equipment of the period when he worked. For example, the unknown Venetian nobleman in this mid-16th-century portrait wears an arming doublet to which relatively small pieces of mail have been laced to protect the man's armpits. These would otherwise have remained vulnerable even after he had put on the plate armour that lies around his feet. (National Gallery, London, England)

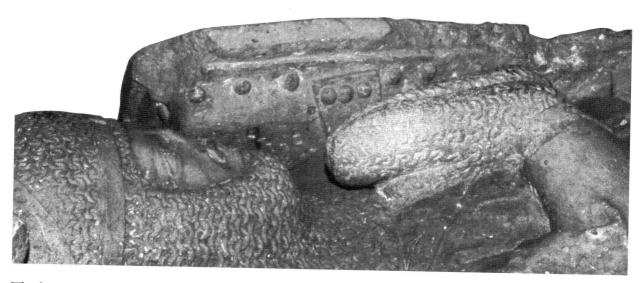

The first comes from an English version of the story of Sir Gawain and the Green Knight dating from around 1370:

Early he calls for his arms, and they all were brought. At first a red carpet was spread on the floor, and there was much gilded gear that gleamed piled upon it. The bold man steps on it and takes the steel in hand. He was arrayed in a doublet of rich fabric of Tarsia, and then a well-made capados, close-fitted, that was lined with light coloured fur. Then they set the sabatons on the man's feet. His legs were enclosed in steel by elegant greaves with attached poleyns. Brightly polished, they were fastened around his knees with golden buckles. Then came the cuisses that snugly enclosed his brawny thighs, attached by means of straps. And afterwards the byrnie, wrought of bright steel rings, enveloped the rich fabric [of the doublet which he already wore]. And they set well burnished vambraces upon both his arms, with good and shiny couters and gauntlets of plate. And all the fine equipment that he needed this time, with splendid coat-armour, his golden spurs proudly fastened on, girt with a trusty sword with a silken belt to his side. When he was fully armoured, his harness was rich, the least buckle and clasps gleamed with gold. (Translated by Helmut Nickel)

Just over 50 years later another English text, the *Worship of Arms* by Johan Hill who was armourer to King Henry VI, described what a gentleman needed either to fight in his sovereign's wars or in this case in a tournament:

First him needeth to have a pair of hose of whipcorde without vampeys. And the said hose cut at the knees and lined within with linen cloth cut on the bias as the

Although medieval sculptors included a substantial amount of realistic detail in their work, they did not always have the technical capabilities to show object in their correct proportions. In this early 14th-century English effigy of Sir Richard de Goldsborough the riveted leather lining and straps of the shield are faithfully represented, though the wooden shield itself is much too thick. (in situ, parish church, Goldsborough, England; David Nicolle)

Effigies carved from wood were more vulnerable than those carved in stone and far fewer survive. On the other hand, those that do still exist sometimes include fine details of arms, armour and costume. The late 13th- or early 14th-century English example seen here even preserves much of the paintwork which is also known to have been applied to stone effigies, though it is likely to have been touched up over the centuries. (in situ, parish church, Fersfield, England; David Nicolle)

hose are. A pair of shoes of red leather laced and fretted underneath with whipcord & persed [given a thin leather sole]. And above within lined with linen cloth three fingers broad, doubled and biased from the toe and anklebone to above the ankle. And so behind at the heel from the sole half a quarter of a yard from this so as to fasten well his sabatons. And the same sabatons fastened under the sole of the foot in two places. Him needeth also a petycote as an overbody of a doublet. His petycote without sleeves, the sizes of it three-quarters around without a collar and reaching no further than the waist and a doublet also with straight sleeves, collar, and certain eyelets on the sleeves for the vambraces and the rerebraces. Armed in this manner, first put on the sabatons, greaves and tight cuisses with voydours of plate or of mail and a close breech [for the groin] of mail with five steel buckles and fine leather straps. And all the arming points after they have been knit and fastened upon him, ensure that the points be cut off [meaning that the remaining lengths of leather laces be removed]. And then a pair of close gussets [of mail], ensuring that the gussets extend three fingers' width within the edges of his plates [cuirass] on both sides. And then a pair of plates of 20 pounds weight on his breast, and these plates secured also with wire or with [leather] points. A pair of rerebraces from within the plates with two forelocks [buckled straps] in the front and three forelocks behind. A pair of vambraces closed with voydours of mail and fretted. A pair of gloves [gauntlets] in whatever style is suitable. A bascinet suited to the lists [tournament] is not suitable for other battle, but when fighting man to man it is said 'necessity hath no law.' The bascinet locked with a bevor and visor which is locked or strapped also to the chest and back with two forelocks. And this aforesaid Gentleman, when he is thus armed and ready to come to the field, will have on him a coat-armour [a tabard at this period] of single cloth which is better when fighting. And his leg harness covered all over with red tarityn [cloth], the which has been called the tincturing of his leg armour because in this manner his opponent will not so easily see his blood. And therefore also his hose should be red for in all other colours the blood will easily be seen. During the olden times in such a battle nothing should have been seen except his helmet and his gauntlets. And finally tie upon him a pair of besagewes [steel discs to protect the shoulder join between the breastplate and the pauldron or rerebrace].

HORSE EQUIPMENT

The horse-harness described in the secular literature of the crusader period tended to be very decorated. That of the Hospitallers was clearly not so. Nevertheless the basic items and elements would have been the same. In the late 12th-century French epic poem *Beatrixe*, for example, the preparation of a warhorse for battle involved putting on and checking the *caignle*, *sorcaingles* and *poitral*, which were the three main straps securing the saddle. The war-saddles

A damaged and little-known 14th-century wall-painting in the cathedral at Bergamo in northern Italy may show grooms at work with a horse or the story of St Martin dividing his cloak with a beggar. It certainly provides an excellent picture a knightly war-saddle from this period. (David Nicolle)

themselves had *arcons* or extensions of the raised cantle or rear of the saddle which went around the lower part of the rider's hips. Under the saddle itself were fine cloth *couvertures*, which were probably saddle-cloths rather than all-enveloping caparisons or bards. Another term for these may have been *senbues*. The seat or cushion of the saddle may have been called a *panel*.

Some degree of decoration was finally allowed on Hospitaller saddles by a statute that was confirmed in 1262. In it Master Hugh Revel stated:

> It is decreed that in the decoration of shields and of saddles and of peytrals there must be no gilding nor silken embroidery but only plain necessary work, except that each brother having a *sella armorum* [war-saddle] may place a little escutcheon [heraldic shield] upon the saddle, and that [the decorations] which were there before might not remain.

Another legal decision reached by the Hospitaller Headquarters in Cyprus during 1303 made a clear distinction between 'Turkish saddles', ordinary riding saddles and war-saddles. 'Turkish saddles' covered in fine *samit* cloth were specifically banned and the regulation also stated that *selles d'armes* or fully developed European style war-saddles must not be used by 'warriors of Syrian origin' because they were turcopoles and not knights.

The gargoyles and other external carvings on medieval churches can only occasionally be viewed from close range. Some of them include interesting details of military costume. Here, a 14th-century figure is armed with a sword and a small round shield or buckler, and clearly wears the sort of thickly quilted soft armour more commonly illustrated in Italian art. (in situ, church of St Mary, Oxford, England; Antoinette Nicolle)

As already stated, horse-armour had been widely used by elite or close-combat cavalry in the Islamic world since at least the 8th century. It did not appear in Western Europe until the late 12th century and then clearly did so as a result of influence from Muslim cavalry in the Iberian peninsula and the Middle East. Such horse-armour remained very expensive, even for the Military Orders, and it seems that armoured horses remained rare within the Crusader States despite the fact that horse-armour became widespread within Western Europe during the late 13th and early 14th centuries.

Another distinctive feature of Italian armour during the 14th century, especially in the south and centre of the country, was an abundant use of decoratively tooled, hardened leather plates to protect the limbs. This was not, of course, confined to Italy, but is well illustrated in this early 14th-century effigy in Salerno. (in situ, cathedral, Salerno, Italy; David Nicolle)

The Hospitallers at War

OPPOSITE

A battle between Hospitallers and Turks in a late 15th-century Hospitaller manuscript. Both forces have landed troops, those of the Christians coming round the left side of the mountain while the Turks come around the right. Meanwhile three Turkish galleys appear to have been trapped inside a bay by two larger Hospitaller warships. Elsewhere the manuscript names some of those who took part, including three English volunteers. (Hours of Pierre de Bosredon, f.140v, MS. Glazier 55, Pierpont Morgan Library; Scala, Florence)

Each Hospitaller brother was expected to go 'on caravan', in other words to do a tour of duty in the East, and some clearly preferred to spend their entire career in active service. In practice, however, it was the younger brethren of military age who tended to be sent to the Middle East or, in later centuries, to the Aegean, while older men remained in the West. Nevertheless, it must be borne in mind that the great majority of these older men, including senior priors and others in Western and Central Europe, had either served as active soldiers earlier in their careers or, as happened in many cases, could still find themselves summoned East to join a garrison in time of crisis. They were by no means soft-living bureaucrats, despite Philip de Mézières' claim that, in the later 14th century, brethren served four or five years in Rhodes simply in order to get a good preceptory or priory when they returned to Europe.

Crusading warfare appears to have been significantly more dangerous than knightly combat in Western Europe, and Military Orders such as the Hospitallers would have expected to suffer consequently higher casualties. In addition, Hospitallers could expect to face enemies and injuries of very different kinds from those experienced in Western Europe; for example, battle against Islamic armies, which relied heavily on archers, resulted in many knights suffering facial wounds. Hospitallers were also particularly vulnerable to loss of horses because of their leading military role.

The idea that the heavily armoured knight dominated the battlefield from the 11th to the 15th centuries was a myth, even within Europe. Such cavalry almost invariably needed the support of infantry. All-cavalry engagements were rare in Western Europe and hardly less so in the crusades. Nevertheless, cavalry did play a more important role in the Middle East, as is reflected in Hospitaller forces of both brethren-in-arms and hired mercenaries. Men on horseback, whether they were heavily armoured cavalry, lighter cavalry or mounted infantry, dominated the raiding that played such a prominent role in crusading warfare.

OPPOSITE (TOP)
The 15th-century barbute was a variation on the salet, or open-faced helmet, which gave greater protection to the face, in this case covering it almost entirely. It was captured by the Ottoman Turks and may have been of Hospitaller origin. (Military Museum, Istanbul, Turkey; David Nicolle)

(BOTTOM)
A typical 15th-century Italian style salet, which extended to protect the neck and sides of the wearer's head. This was the most common form of helmet used in the European Mediterranean and would have been standard equipment amongst the Hospitallers of Rhodes. This particular example, having been captured by the Turks, might well have been taken from Hospitallers somewhere in the Aegean region. (Military Museum, Istanbul, Turkey; David Nicolle)

CAMPAIGNING AND BATTLES ON LAND

Where the Military Orders were concerned, a crusading campaign would begin with the brethren mustering in their quarters with their horses, pack-animals and livestock to provide food 'on the hoof'. At this stage they were under the command of the Marshal but would often be transferred to the command of the Gonfalonier as the raid set out. On both raids and larger campaigns the force might find itself involved in a 'fighting march', that is, it might be harassed by enemy forces while on the move. The techniques of such a fighting march had already been highly developed by both Byzantine and Islamic armies, while the Military Orders became famous for their abilities in such engagements during the 12th century. When larger armies were on the move the Hospitallers and Templars often provided essential vanguards and rearguards. The Hospitallers were in the rearguard at the battle of Arsuf in 1191.

The Rule of the Templars provides more detailed information than that of the Hospitallers, but they are likely to have operated in much the same manner. For example, when a force was preparing to march, the brother-knights assembled ahead with the squires who followed with the baggage. Once they were ready to move the squires rode ahead with the knights' weapons and spare horses. Secular sources indicate that the raising of banners was a signal for an army or caravan to set off. A Hospitaller statute of 1263 stated that a caravan or raid was normally led by the Master, his Lieutenant, the Marshal or the Commander of Knights. The force was usually accompanied by priests, probably from the Order itself, and there was to be no looting by individuals, all booty being assembled collectively. In hostile territory the brother-knights held their shields and when they came near to the enemy they put on their helmets. In friendly territory, however, these shields were carried by squires or servants, though the fighting men probably wore their helmets even here.

Once again the Hospitallers are likely to have obeyed similar regulations to the Templars, amongst whom it was insisted that if a man wanted to change position while on the march, he must do so downwind from the main body to avoid sending dust into their eyes. In peacetime men could water their horses at passing streams, but in enemy country they were only to do so when the Gonfalonier signalled a halt. If the alarm sounded, those closest to the emergency were to take up their weapons and await orders, while those further away should muster around the Master for his orders.

Much the same was expected if an encampment was attacked. Those nearest the threat were required to take a spear and shield and to hurry to repel the threat, while others mustered in the chapel-tent to await orders. On campaign the Military Orders erected their tents around a chapel-tent, in which all their equipment was stored while the servants foraged for firewood and water, though the servants were not to go beyond earshot of the camp's bell. The Gonfalonier shouted orders in camp or on the march, and was also responsible for distributing fodder for the horses. Food for the men was distributed communally according to status, with brother-knights eating separately from brother-sergeants. Templars ate in pairs, but whether the Hospitallers also did so is unknown.

Hospitallers were involved in all sorts of medieval warfare, from skirmishes to full-scale battles and sieges both offensive and defensive. Imad al-Din al-Isfahani described one such skirmish between Saladin's reconnaissance units and a crusader force from Saffuriyah, adding the strange and perhaps merely poetic observation that as the crusaders charged, 'The Templars were humming like bees, the Hospitallers bellowing like the wind'. Even the best-equipped and trained crusader cavalryman could be vulnerable to determined infantry when operating in broken or hilly terrain. The chronicler and crusader Jean de Joinville stated that the *couvertures* or protective coverings of crusader cavalry horses were pulled off by enemy footsoldiers so that the latter could strike the animals themselves. Other sources show that light cavalry turcopoles of the Military Orders were similarly effective in rough country, being better able to manoeuvre rapidly in an emergency.

Large forces of European knightly cavalry were capable of moving in a co-ordinated manner, and in general there was remarkable similarity between descriptions of such manoeuvres and those of tactical movements in Byzantine-Greek and Arab-Islamic military manuals. For example, the early to mid-12th-century Anglo-Norman writer Wace described an army advancing in close order:

> Those on foot led the way, in serried ranks bearing bows. The knights rode close, protecting the archers from behind. Those on horse and those on foot, just as they had begun, kept their order and the same pace, in close ranks and at a slow march, so that no-one might overtake another, nor get too close nor too far apart. All advanced in close order, and all advanced bravely.

Great discipline was required of crusader armies because their tactics, which proved to be more cumbersome than those of most Islamic forces, normally left the initiative to their foes. Consequently crusader armies often endured constant pin-prick attacks and under such circumstances the steadiness of the Hospitallers, not least in providing an example to their less experienced colleagues, must have been invaluable. Templar sources again provide greater detail. Once an army was arrayed no man could leave his position in the ranks unless it was to test his horse and saddle, or to help a comrade in distress. He must then immediately return to his proper position. If a man wanted to speak to the Master he must go on foot and then return to his own place, perhaps because riding off on horseback might look like retreating and thus cause alarm. On campaign the Military Orders operated in *eschielles* or squadrons under nominated leaders, while the Gonfalonier had another small unit to guard him and his flag. An eschielle was apparently smaller than a conrois, though the term conrois may only have referred to a tactical rather than organizational unit. Each conrois seems to have numbered from 20 to 40 men drawn up in two or three ranks. Several conrois drawn up in line normally formed up a *bataille* or battlefield division.

Hospitaller forces often came up against Turco-Mongol-style horse-archers during this period. Yet most modern commentators on crusader warfare have tended to exaggerate the tactical effectiveness of such horse-archery when compared to European tactics of the time. In reality, the short composite bows used by Turks,

A relatively simple illustration of a siege, this time from mid-14th-century Spain. It shows an assault upon a fortress whose stone walls have additional timber defences on top. The weaponry ranges from sophisticated crossbows to simple javelins and even stones thrown by hand. (Avila Bible; f.476, Liria Palace, Madrid, Spain)

Though this picture in a late 13th-century manuscript from Acre illustrates Joseph going to Egypt, it also provides a clear impression of the sort of camel transport used by the Hospitallers and other armies in the Middle East. (Histoire Universelle, f.57r, MS. 562, Bibliothèque Municipale, Dijon, France)

Mongols and Mamluk armies had limitations. Lightly equipped horse-archers were particularly vulnerable if forced into close combat with more heavily armoured men. Though the maximum range of the Turkish bow was very large, its killing range was short because its relatively light arrows could carry far but lacked impact. These arrows could be effective against a large target like a horse, which might be injured or panicked, but were less so against men on foot, particularly if the latter were protected by large shields and were armed with crossbows. It is also possible that crossbowmen overcame the slow rate of shooting of their weapons by loosing concentrated volleys when the more lightly equipped Islamic horse-archers came close. It also seems clear that a substantial proportion of infantry in the Crusader States, including Hospitaller brother-sergeants and professional mercenaries, was heavily armoured. One tactical problem with crossbows, however, was that Islamic cavalry tended to withdraw out of range as soon as they saw crusader infantry place their feet in the stirrups of their weapons, preparatory to spanning and loading them.

An almost perfectly preserved 15th-century Spanish brigandine or scale-lined cuirass. This form was particularly popular amongst men serving on foot or at sea because, while still providing good protection, the brigandine was relatively light and flexible. (Museo Militar, Madrid, Spain)

When facing armoured cavalry in close formation, horse-archers had to disrupt the enemy's cohesion, prompt a precipitate charge or lure the cavalry away from their defensive infantry through feigned flight. The renowned discipline of the Hospitallers made them less vulnerable to horse-archers than most other Western European cavalry, particularly when Hospitaller cavalry were operating in close co-operation with similarly disciplined infantrymen. For this reason, reliable infantry, especially crossbowmen, were perhaps more important at an earlier date in the Crusader States than they were within Europe.

BATTLEFIELD TACTICS

The essentially defensive battlefield tactics that resident crusader forces, including those of the Military Orders, developed were virtually identical to those of Arab-Islamic armies, which leaves the fascinating possibility that the Hospitallers and other Middle Eastern Military Orders actually learned a great deal from 12th-century Fatimid and Ayyubid forces.

A cavalry charge by an armoured conrois tended to react to the actions of its Saracen or Turkish foe, thus leaving the tactical initiative to the Muslims. Nevertheless, the organization of such a charge was more complex than might be thought. On campaign the Gonfalonier arranged squadrons of squires with spare war-horses who would ride behind the brother-knights as the latter charged. Other squires with the riding horses remained close to the Gonfalonier's banner. The turcopoles were similarly organized into squadrons under a brother-knight and they too could charge behind the knights in case the latter needed assistance. Brother-sergeants sometimes charged with the knights and formed a second supporting rank. It was important for the horses in a charge to remain very close together and in close touch with their banner.

The charge itself was not fast, probably only at a trot and then perhaps spurring into a canter just before impact, though even this is unlikely as a horse will not normally crash into what appears to be a fixed obstacle. A mêlée or close combat normally followed if the charge actually struck its target, which by no means always happened. There was also the serious danger of an ill-considered charge itself being hit in the flank or rear by enemy cavalry. In Europe the main tactical role of a charge was to break the enemy line, then wheel and attack again from the back. However, in Europe the enemy was usually static or slow-moving infantry or comparably cumbersome cavalry. By comparison, in the Middle East, suitable targets for a cavalry charge were extremely rare, so it is hardly surprising to learn that one of the primary roles of brother-sergeants was to hold off the enemy if their brother-knights suffered a reverse or were unable to reform. The failure of an armoured cavalry charge could have catastrophic consequences, hence the vital role of formations of infantry archers and crossbowmen to provide a safe haven, and of more nimble turcopoles to guard the charge's flanks and rear.

In the mêlée that was expected to follow a charge, no man was supposed to leave his position even if wounded, though he could send someone else, perhaps a servant, to seek permission from the commander to withdraw. Both Christian and Muslim sources make it clear that it was difficult to knock an armoured Western knight from his saddle, as the mid-13th century *Seljuk-Namah* by Ibn Bibi revealed:

> The Frank descended upon him with his lance levelled. The Sultan [Kaikhusrau] parried the blow with his shield and evaded a second shock. At the third pass he struck a terrible blow with his mace surmounted by a bull's head at the Frank worshipper of the hoof of Jesus's donkey... The Frank's horse had not been able to evade the mace-blow at its rider who was solidly attached to the saddle and he remained suspended, unconscious and senseless.

Consequently Islamic soldiers were trained to attack the enemy's horses rather than the riders. Abu Shama described the results of this training at the battle of Hattin:

> A Frankish knight, as long as his horse was in good condition, could not be knocked down. Covered with mail from head to foot, which made him look like a block of iron, the most violent blows make no impression on him. But once his horse was killed, the knight was thrown and taken prisoner. Consequently though we counted them [Frankish prisoners] by the thousand, there were no horses amongst the spoils whereas the knights were unhurt. The horse had to be felled by spear or sword to bring down the knight from his saddle.

It was vital for brethren-in-arms not to become scattered and vulnerable, hence the supreme importance of standards as rallying points for the men in the confusion and dust of battle. Several Military Orders had regulations stating how a man should rally to the banner of another Order, indeed any Christian banner, if his own banner fell. This would certainly have been true of the Hospitallers.

A detail of the scale-lined interior of a 15th-century English brigandine armour. It is worth noting that the size and shape of the iron scales varied according to what part of the body they were covering. (Castle Museum, Warwick, England; David Nicolle)

163

CASTLES AND SIEGE WARFARE

Hospitaller castles served the same function as other crusader fortifications. In the early days they were primarily used as bases for offensive operations, though they also served as places of refuge. In the later years, though such castles could not actually plug an invasion route or even close a strategic pass, they did provide defence in depth because their garrisons could threaten an invader's communications or supply lines. Many of the most impressive Hospitaller castles are located in rugged areas where they are difficult to reach even today. Although they were by no means invulnerable, such locations made these castles difficult to bombard with contemporary siege machines. However, Muslim rulers usually enjoyed a considerable superiority in the number of foot soldiers available to them, if not of elite or professional troops. Such infantry could harass and eventually wear down the defenders, both physically and morally, by repeated small assaults on different sections of the wall.

Siege warfare was vitally important to the Hospitallers. According to Abbot Guibert de Nogent, writing in the early 12th century, knights were assigned to wooden siege towers so that they could fight the similarly well-armoured men defending the walls opposite them. This put the knights in a dangerous position as they were exposed to archery, crossbows and javelins, which could pierce armour at short range. When defending a fortification a Hospitaller garrison made the usual use of sorties, though not necessarily by knights. For example, during Saladin's attack on the Hospitaller castle of Belvoir the garrison sent out a sortie by 200 crossbowmen described as 'skilled in mountain warfare', because Belvoir was in a rugged location. During the Mamluks' final siege of Acre in

This distinctive polygonal artillery bastion is in the western wall of Rhodes city. It was built around an earlier and taller round tower during the 15th century and its gunnery embrasures are at ground level, being designed to shoot down enemies who entered the dry moat. (David Nicolle)

A light field cannon shown in a scene of battle on a Flemish tapestry dating from the 15th century. The gunner shields his face from the flash as he places the heated torch to the gun's touch-hole. (Castle Museum, Saumur, France; David Nicolle)

1291 both the Hospitallers and the Templars made large-scale sorties against the enemy's left and right flanks, though with little success.

Sorties from castles and raids launched from the same castles had much in common. For example, in 1188 raiders from the Hospitaller garrison of Belvoir intercepted one of Saladin's supply trains carrying weaponry, food and other materials from the recently captured Templar castle at La Fève. Some years later in 1213 the Hospitallers merely had to threaten a major raid for the Islamic city of Hama to pay a substantial amount to buy them off. Later Hospitaller attempts to use the same raiding strategy were less successful unless the Muslim defenders were preoccupied elsewhere, as happened during a Mongol invasion of Syria in 1281.

Though some Hospitaller garrisons endured prolonged sieges, others collapsed remarkably quickly, sometimes almost without a fight; a special decree issued in 1283, stating that no Hospitaller castle could surrender without first informing the Master, suggests that such a thing had already happened at least once. The psychological aspects of medieval siege warfare have rarely been studied, but the emphasis that the Hospitallers placed upon communications suggests that they were fully aware of the danger of such garrisons feeling abandoned. This was where

Another episode during the defeat of the Ottoman siege of Rhodes in 1480 involved the collapse of a floating bridge that the Turks had built across part of the harbour. (Obsidionis Rhodie Urbis Descriptio by William Caoursin; akg-images)

carrier pigeons came into their own. The crusaders had copied the Muslims' highly developed pigeon-postal system by the 1120s and the Hospitallers also adopted the idea. A letter written by Jacques de Vitry in 1217 explained how pigeons were used when the 'Assassins' threatened the Hospitaller castle of Crac des Chevaliers: 'When on account of our fear of the pagans we would not dare to send messengers, we used to send pigeons carrying our letters under their wings to summon men of the city to us'. Another reference in a Scottish source described how in 1266 a Hospitaller raid won considerable booty from the Mamluks: 'And the brothers of the Hospital sent to the Hospital [their headquarters in Acre] their pigeon with a letter concerning their deed.' This message was, however, premature as the raiders were ambushed on their way home.

The 15th- and 16th-century European military elite clearly had no objection to the use of firearms, despite the fulminations of some chivalric writers who bemoaned the supposedly more gentlemanly warfare of an earlier age. These new weapons included handguns as well as cannon for siege and naval warfare. This was equally true of the Hospitallers. In fact, the failed Mamluk siege of Rhodes in 1444 is said to have been the model for the sieges in *Tirant lo Blanc* by the Catalan writer Martorell. Hospitaller naval warfare, as described by Catalans and others who returned to Spain, may similarly have been the model for a naval battle in the same book.

Martorell's epic story describes how soldiers were ordered to sleep in their armour and to expect battle early the following day, to use the battle-axe as the most effective weapon against heavily armoured opponents in close combat and to use a light form of crossbow on horseback while making a sortie from the fortifications. Within the besieged city, theft was to be avoided by having half the houses hang lanterns in their windows until midnight, and the rest of the houses hanging lanterns from midnight until dawn. Countermines beneath the walls were said to be filled with brass bowls, which rattled if enemy miners were using pick-axes nearby. The defenders then fired cannon into an enemy tunnel that had broken through beneath their fortifications. Finally, vats or pans filled with chopped goats' hair and mutton fat were lit at midnight, causing the stench of burning animals to blow across the enemy camp and stampede their terrified flocks.

The concern for livestock was clearly a feature of Hospitaller Rhodes. During the first Ottoman siege of 1480 the Turcopolier, traditionally an English brother, and his turcopoles were responsible for gathering flocks, herds and available supplies of grain into the safety of the city. The Turcopolier was also in charge of coastal defences, observation and signalling. Presumably turcopoles as well as brother-knights, brother-sergeants and other troops would have taken part in the sorties that attacked the surrounding Ottoman siege works, following which the heads of dead Turks were paraded around the fortifications.

NAVAL AND ISLAND WARFARE

Following the fall of Acre in 1291 it gradually became clear that crusading warfare against the Mamluks in the eastern Mediterranean would henceforth be primarily naval. The fall of the Templar-held island of Ruad and the Mamluk defeat of the Mongols, followed by the latter's conversion to Islam, effectively marked the end of crusader attempts to retake the Holy Land. Instead, the Hospitallers initially favoured a series of small campaigns against the Mamluks, known as *passage particulier*, rather than another all-out crusading assault or *passage général*. What the Hospitaller Master proposed was that a force of 1,000 knights and 4,000 crossbowmen should be raised to serve for five years and that it should be supported by a fleet of 60 galleys based in Rhodes, which were to take to sea for eight months each year. He even suggested that an overland trade route to India and the Far East be developed in order to divert transit trade away from Egypt and thus undermine the Mamluk Sultanate's economy. It was a remarkably sophisticated concept and indicated just how modern the Hospitaller hierarchy was in its strategic thinking. However, its implementation remained beyond the military capabilities of Western Europe at the time.

There were also problems with the idea of imposing a naval blockade upon Egypt. Cyprus was normally five or six days' sailing from Egypt; Rhodes was even further. Fleets were frequently scattered by storms, and the need to confine major naval operations to the fair weather of summer meant that food and water deteriorated rapidly. It was similarly difficult to maintain the health of armies if they had to remain in one place too long. All these problems and strategic limitations contributed to a shift in Hospitaller strategy during the 14th century. They turned

OPPOSITE
The aftermath of the defeat of the Ottoman siege of Rhodes in 1480, with Turkish dead outside the walls. Some of the towers show considerable damage, while groups of four cannon have been placed on raised batteries made of timber and earth. (Obsidionis Rhodie Urbis Descriptio by William Caoursin, f.79v, MS. Lat. 6067, Bibliothèque Nationale, Paris, France; The Bridgeman Art Library)

A 15th-century French manuscript illustration of the ancient Greek legend of the Argonauts, who are seen here landing at Colchis, gives some idea of how a medieval army made a beach-landing in hostile territory. Written sources indicate that the role of trumpeters in the stern of such a ship would have been to recall those who had gone ashore. (f.31, MS. Douce 353, Bodleian Library, Oxford, England; 2004 Topham Picturepoint)

By the later medieval period the Hospitallers were highly experienced in naval warfare and they also enthusiastically adopted cannon in the 15th century. The naval gun shown here was actually found in the sea off the English coast near Harwich and dates from the second half of the 15th century. Essentially the same weapons would have been used aboard Hospitaller vessels in the Mediterranean. (Historical Museum, Colchester, England; David Nicolle)

away from the eastern Mediterranean to the Aegean. The Hospitallers even started to play a part in the defence of the Latin-Crusader States on mainland Greece. In 1375 they proposed a Crusade to consist of almost 400 brethren with their squires: 125 from the French priories, 108 from the Italian, 73 from the Iberian, 38 from the English and Irish, 32 from the German and Bohemian, 17 from Hungary and two each from the preceptories of Morea and Athens. In the event the Order failed to assemble anywhere near this number and the proposal was a flop.

Rhodes and the south-eastern Aegean remained their primary consideration. On land there was very little fighting with the Turks during the late 14th and early 15th centuries, except skirmishes that merely provoked enemy reprisals. The navy of the Order had, meanwhile, evolved into an elite corps. Even so it remained small, consisting on average of only four war-galleys, and so could not conduct significant independent actions. Instead it was held ready for joint action with other Western European fleets. The Hospitallers' ships were responsible for the maritime defence of Rhodes and the other islands and after Izmir fell to Timur-i-Lenk in 1402 an enlarged Hospitaller navy turned its attention to persistent and piratical raiding of Ottoman commerce. The massive new castle at Bodrum on the site of the ancient Hellenistic city of Halicarnassus now gave the Hospitallers a new outpost on the Turkish mainland following the loss of Izmir. It was erected in territory claimed by the beylik of Mentese and, with the Hospitaller-held offshore islands, enabled Christian galleys to attack passing merchant ships almost at will.

The Hospitallers maintained their corsair warfare in what they regarded as a naval crusade against the Ottomans and which their victims, as well as the Venetians, saw as piracy. In return, the Turks launched almost annual naval raids against Rhodes or the other islands, seeking to undermine the Hospitaller economy by cutting down orchards or vineyards, burning farm buildings, and seizing livestock and captives who were then resettled on the mainland. Most raids were in April or May and at one point so many oxen had been taken that ploughing became difficult. As a result, Hospitaller fortifications were strengthened and many small towers were built as refuges for local people and their animals. The Hospitaller Master meanwhile had spies in Gallipoli, the main Ottoman naval base, and there was usually a Hospitaller patrol boat in the region that would race back to Rhodes with a warning if the Ottoman fleet emerged.

Tension remained high, with the Master assembling his troops in expectation of major Ottoman assaults every year from 1477 to 1480, when the attack at last came. In fact, the Sultan sent only a part of his army against Rhodes because he was campaigning on several other fronts; nevertheless, the Hospitaller fleet did not intercept the enemy at sea. Instead it was held back, probably to maintain communications with the outside world and in case a counter-attack proved possible.

The Order's greatest naval success in the early 16th century was the destruction of a Mamluk fleet in the Gulf of Iskenderun in 1510. Here the Master had advised his naval commander to fight 'discreetly like wise and experienced men, and bravely like knights and gentlemen assigned to the defence of the Holy Faith'. However, this unprovoked attack proved a strategic disaster because it destroyed the traditionally good relations between the Hospitallers and the Mamluks. Seven years later the Mamluk Sultanate of Egypt and Syria was itself conquered by the Ottomans.

Despite the cult of chivalry and knighthood encouraged in Hospitaller Rhodes, almost all the fighting seen by the brethren was either at sea, or attacking coastal positions, or in defence of their own fortifications. Paradoxically, perhaps, some of the best accounts of Hospitallers at war are found in Turkish. For example, the *Destan of Umur Pasha*, written in the mid-15th century, describes the Hospitallers and other crusaders attacking a Turkish position outside Izmir a century earlier:

In the morning the enemy put on their cuirasses and arms. Their horse-armour, their cuirasses were amazing. Their gauntlets, their arm-defences, their leg defences, their helmets, all shone and twinkled in the light. Those who carried small crossbows came in front, those who carried large crossbows and arrows followed. There were an infinite number carrying javelins and shields, and as numerous were those with swords and daggers. The drums, the cymbals and the trumpets sounded. They surged up from the sea and made their assault. In the wink of an eye they reached the ditch. They carried fire to burn the mangonels. They wielded very long axes and broke all the palisades in the ditch.

An astonishing assembly of diverse pieces of armour was found in part of the fortifications of Rhodes during the late 19th century. Most was not particularly high quality and would now be called 'munitions' armour. What was equally interesting was the fact that it had been made in virtually all the known centres of 15th-century European arms manufacture, indicating that the Hospitallers acquired military equipment from wherever they could. (Bachereau Sale Rooms, Paris, France)

Battle between Greeks and Amazons led by Hippolyta, in a French-Burgundian manuscript of the Theseide by the Italian poet Boccaccio, made around 1470. Once again a fleet is shown landing an army on an enemy coast and in the face of stiff opposition. The picture also highlights the importance of archers to provide covering fire while small boats transfer troops from ship to the beach. (MS. 2617, Nat. Bib., Vienna, Austria; akg-images/Nimatallah)

Yet the Order's primary military concern from the later 14th century on remained naval warfare, which had always been dominated by technology. War-galleys themselves changed from the late 13th to mid-14th centuries from a system whereby one oarsman pulled one oar, though these were usually grouped into three sitting on a single bench, to a system in which from five to seven oarsmen pulled a single much larger oar. The difference between strict war-galleys and those galleys which carried high-value cargoes was similarly increasing. By the later 15th century it was traditional for Hospitaller galleys to be noticeably larger than those of other fleets, except some from Venice. This enabled them to keep the seas for a longer period and in worse weather, sometimes even through winter.

Rhodes itself had sufficient timber to repair if not to construct many ships, most of which were built in Genoa or Marseilles. Even so, the Order had to

have materials sent to Rhodes. In the late 15th century, for example, the Master ordered the Hospitaller Commander of Savona in Italy to send two galleys and their crews, plus '400 pieces of cotton cloth, 200 for sails for galleys and 200 for [merchant] ships, 300 oars, and ropes and hawsers for two galleys'. The naval arsenal in Rhodes was called the Tersenal and as it was normal for Aegean galleys to be taken out of the water during winter, this was probably also true within the Tersenal. Otherwise galleys and merchant ships were moored in the main harbour, but not in the neighbouring Mandraccio cove as was once thought.

The Hospitaller Admiral was in charge of all the Order's galleys and of any other ordinary ships that had been armed for war, along with their crews. He could also hire additional galleys whose crews and marines would be paid by the Order's Treasury. However, the Admiral, and the fighting men, were under the command of the Marshal if he accompanied the fleet. Following a landing, the knights were placed under the Commander of Knights. Finally, the Master could license an ordinary Hospitaller brother either to 'arm' or to provision a galley or other ship at their own expense, this being particularly common in the 15th century.

Very little information seems to survive concerning the armament aboard Hospitaller ships, but it is likely to have been much the same as that aboard vessels from elsewhere, at least when the latter were operating in Aegean waters. For example Venetian galleys in the 14th-century Aegean or eastern Mediterranean carried 30 to 50 men armed with swords, ten to 16 with crossbows, or even 20 such crossbowmen in times of particular danger. Merchant ships and galleys often carried large 'two-feet' and smaller 'one-foot' crossbows, sometimes two weapons for each fully qualified crossbowman.

Other regulations stipulated the armour and even the type of armour to be carried. Genoese naval regulations of around 1330, which are likely to have been similar to Hospitaller practice, insisted that a galley with a crew of 176 men included junior officers and 12 crossbowmen. Eight of the latter also served as

Under Hospitaller rule, the island of Rhodes was dotted with castles, most of which were close to the coast. The example at Monolithos has a particularly dramatic location, perched on a tall rocky outcrop that hardly needed a curtain wall to make it defensible. (David Nicolle)

oarsmen while four were considered specialists with two weapons each. The ship was also 'armed' with 160 cuirasses, 160 gorgets (plated throat protection), 170 helmets, 12 other crossbows, 5,000 crossbow bolts, plus spears, javelins and bills. No other edged weapons were listed, so the crew probably provided their own. The ship's captain, who would be a specific target for enemy sharpshooters, was expected to have heavier armour than the other men, consisting of a cuirass that had been *proofed*, or tested under controlled conditions, an iron gorget, a proofed helmet, a good sword, *pavise* (large shield), dagger and iron gauntlets. The ship's scribe had the same armour as the captain, whereas the *nauclerius* or sailing master had less. By 1483–84, according to Felix Faber, a 15th-century Dominican who travelled to Palestine, the weaponry aboard a pilgrim galley included cannon and handbows, probably of composite construction.

In tall merchant ships and in low-lying galleys the prow and stern were the most strongly defended parts of the vessel, with the mid-ships remaining relatively vulnerable. In galleys it was the forecastle that above all formed the focus of defence and attack, this being where most of the armoured men were stationed. The stone-throwing mangonels sometimes recorded aboard ship are likely to have been carried for use on shore, or at best during an attack on a coastal fortification. The image of great stones being hurled from one vessel against another is largely mythical.

For Hospitallers service aboard ship was still called 'caravan' and was obligatory for all brethren. The brother-knights would, however, almost always

The Hospitallers built their castle of St Peter at Bodrum on the Turkish mainland to replace Izmir (Smyrna) which had been lost, firstly to Timur-i-Lenk and then to the Turks. Its location on a long and almost uninhabited peninsula, and its command of an excellent harbour, made this fortress a major strategic asset in the naval warfare of the 15th-century Aegean. (David Nicolle)

175

have been in positions of responsibility. As such they could find themselves in command of motley crews. The pool of sailors, oarsmen and naval troops in the Aegean region included Russians, Italians, Greeks, Spaniards and assorted peoples from the Black Sea coast. Then there were the Hospitallers' own subjects from Rhodes, plus various slaves. By the later 15th century two-thirds of the oarsmen were slaves, mostly Muslims, while the *buonavoglia* (volunteers) already included a remarkable number of Maltese long before the Hospitallers took over that island.

Naval tactics were based upon raiding enemy coasts and ambushing his merchant ships. The relatively small galiote, with 12 to 22 rowing benches, was best for raiding. Larger galleys may often have been used to ambush sailing ships, particularly as the latter tended to increase in bulk and height during the 14th and 15th centuries as a way of protecting themselves against pirate attack. Strong local knowledge was a major reason for the success and high reputation of Hospitaller galleys. This was obviously necessary when, as was usually the case, two galleys worked together. One would lie in wait behind a headland or small island while the second harried the victim into the jaws of this ambush. It should be pointed out that almost all shipping lanes lay along the coasts, with deep-water voyaging relatively rare. When the Hospitallers did meet an enemy at sea they would have used traditional boarding tactics, usually relying upon the raised *calcar* (beak) rather than the ship-breaking ram which now formed the prow of a Mediterranean galley.

Coastal raids could involve substantially larger forces, and if an enemy fortification was to be attacked then crossbowmen would play a primary role. *Tirant lo Blanc* by Martorell again offers a vivid picture, with a flotilla of galleys approaching in very close formation so that they all hit the beach at roughly the same time. Even so, the ships still had to turn and then backwater because raiding parties disembark from the stern, not from the prow as in a modern landing craft. The *Destan of Umur Pasha*, written in Turkish around the same time, described just such a descent upon Izmir harbour by crusaders, Hospitallers and others. 'Thirty galleys were sent to Izmir, all filled with men in full armour... These innumerable Franks were dressed in iron from head to foot.' During a subsequent attack upon Izmir town, 'Many coats of mail, shields, cuirasses and helmets were made in the lands of these enemies. They took also swords, javelins and daggers. They wanted to form an army, they took also the great crossbows and small crossbows, bows, arrows and hand-guns. They built many galleys.' In a later verse the Turkish poet described the sound of these hand-guns or *tüfeks* in battle: 'Shat! Shat!'

When beached stern first, a flotilla of galleys was in a strong defensive position if threatened from the sea. Battles between fleets at sea were, however, rare.

OPPOSITE
King Louis IX lands at Damietta during the Sixth Crusade, as illustrated in a 15th-century biography of the French king who, though disastrously unsuccessful as a crusader, was eventually declared to be a saint. The white crosses on a red ground worn by the soldiers who precede him down the ramp may identify them as Hospitallers. (Livres des Faits de Monseigneur Saint Louis; f.36v, MS. Fr. 2829, Bibliothèque Nationale de France, Paris)

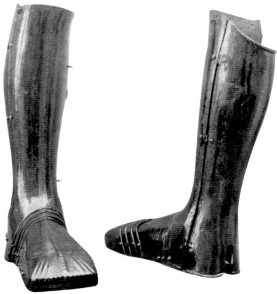

References to ships being linked by cables only seemed to occur in harbour or in very enclosed waters, and even then they were not tied closely to one another as Viking ships once were. Normally such galleys formed a loose line with larger transport galleys and sailing ships in reserve, while small vessels carried messages between ships. These tactics were rarely necessary for the Hospitallers because their Turkish foes tended to use large numbers of smaller ships in rapid raiding operations, though they were rarely capable of taking on bigger Christian galleys. Furthermore, the rulers of rival Turkish beyliks rarely co-operated to form larger fleets, which only appeared when the Ottomans took control of the entire Anatolian coast. Even then the early Ottoman navy was designed for raiding or for transporting the land forces that conquered the Aegean islands one by one.

Such a disparity between the sizes, numbers and tactics of Christian and Islamic warships is again reflected in *Tirant lo Blanc*. Netting was sometimes suspended over the decks to protect against rocks or heavy iron bars that might be dropped from above and, of course, to inhibit boarding. The waist and forecastle of the ship could be padded with all available mattresses against early cannon while the arrows that stuck in masts and rigging might make it impossible to lower the sails. Bombards or larger cannon on these ships were only loaded when the enemy was near and small ships could be rigged to look like bigger vessels to frighten an enemy. Armour was taken from the wounded during the battle so that it could be used by others, and after a victory the enemy dead and wounded were both tipped into the sea.

The size of Christian ships clearly impressed the author of the Turkish *Destan of Umur Pasha* who wrote that 'their topsails are like fortresses. The cogs carry enemies without number.' The 15th-century Turkish use of the term *kuka* or *cog* applied to a more sophisticated ship than the Northern European cogs from which the word was taken. It may have meant the singularly large carracks which, from the late 15th century onwards, were used by the Hospitallers of both Rhodes and subsequently Malta in combination with their already large galleys. The biggest was called a great carrack and would operate in support of two or more galleys, providing the supplies which enabled the latter to raid much further afield. The first was mentioned in 1478, though the most famous was probably an Egyptian ship called the *Mogarbina* (probably originally Arabic *al-Maghribiya* meaning 'the North African one') that the Hospitallers captured in 1507. She remained in Hospitaller service even after the Order moved to Malta.

The Hospitallers' biggest and most ambitious great carrack was laid down at Nice during the same year that the Order lost Rhodes. This was the *Santa Anna* which, launched in 1524, was a remarkable vessel by any standards and became the most powerful fighting vessel in the Mediterranean. She had four masts, 3,000 tonnes displacement, the first metal-sheathed bottom known in Europe, two gun decks, 50 large cannon and many smaller, an armoury for 500 soldiers and 100 brother-knights, and provisions for six months at sea. In addition to a large bakery, other ovens and stoves, the *Santa Anna* was even said to carry a 'grove' of cypress trees and some mandarin orange trees! She was like a floating palace for the Master and his court. Though successful in several engagements, the *Santa Anna* suffered from the teething troubles faced by most ambitious prototypes and was hugely expensive to operate. As a result she was laid up during the Hospitallers' financial crisis in 1540 before eventually being broken up. From then on the Order commissioned a new but ordinary galleon, or warship relying on sail power, every 12 to 15 years.

OPPOSITE TOP

Another piece of armour found in a cache of discarded Hospitaller military equipment in Rhodes. This particular breastplate and the fauld which protected the wearer's hips is believed to have been made in northern Italy and dates from the very early 16th century. (T. Richardson)

OPPOSITE BOTTOM

A pair of decorated greaves and sabatons used by a senior Hospitaller brother and bearing the maker's mark of the Missaglia factory in northern Italy. This was perhaps the most prestigious armour-manufacturing company of the day and these particular leg defences are believed to date from around 1525. (Armoury of the Knights of St John. Malta; G.F. Laking)

Sickness, Death and Remembrance

OPPOSITE

Hospitaller troops manning the walls of the city of Rhodes during the Ottoman Turkish siege in 1480. Note that the crossbowman on the left does not wear the red tabard and cross of the Order, and might represent a mercenary employed by the Military Order. (Obsidionis Rhodie Urbis Descriptio by William Caoursin, f.55v, MS. Lat. 6067, Bibliothèque Nationale de France, Paris)

Old or sick Hospitaller brethren were excused ordinary duties and fasts, but not punishment when they broke the rules. Only the Master could give permission for the infirm or aged to hand in their arms. Meanwhile, those who became lepers were not allowed to live with other brethren but were still fed and clothed. Other sick or injured brethren needed specific permission from their superior before they could be bled, and this not more than once a week on Saturday. There was an infirmary for those more seriously ill in the East before 1206, while comparable infirmaries were subsequently attached to larger commanderies, separate from conventual buildings but close to the church. If an individual's sickness persisted beyond a certain time he was sent to an infirmary, but before this he was simply confined to his bed in the dorter, dormitory or cell.

Permission to go to the infirmary was only given reluctantly. The sick man then took his own bed and his military equipment to the infirmary, where he confessed his sins, stated whether he was a creditor or a debtor, and whether he had anything that was not his own. He was then helped to draw up an inventory of his goods, was given the sacraments, and handed over any keys of office to his prior. Thereafter the sick person had to ask permission to leave the infirmary to go to the public baths or a place of recreation. He was forbidden to play chess, read romances, or eat prohibited food. A special refectory was attached to the infirmary, which prepared similar food to that eaten by healthy brethren, though it was eaten before other brothers had their meals. It may also have included a broader choice of food or cooking methods as well as better 'house wine'. Brothers who had been medically bled that week were also allowed to eat in the infirmary.

Epidemics of plague were a regular hazard in the eastern Mediterranean regions and these tended to hit foreigners worse than they did local or indigenous

A surgeon putting a splint around a patient's broken leg, as illustrated in a 13th-century medical treatise. The idea that medieval doctors were ignorant and brutish is clearly nonsense, and the evidence shows that they were often remarkably successful given the limited knowledge and basic conditions of the time. (Livres de Cyrurgie of Roger of Parma, f.9r, MS. Sloane 1977, British Library, London, England)

inhabitants. Hence crusaders, Military Orders and their Mamluk foes on the Islamic side of the frontier all suffered badly. Pestilence carried off many Hospitaller brother-knights in Rhodes in the later 14th century, shortly before the equally disastrous Crusade of Nicopolis. Information from the 14th to early 16th centuries shows that the treatment of sick brethren and the system for dealing with their effects or insignia of office had not changed much since earlier days, though more detail is now available. For example, when a brother in the central convent fell seriously ill his prior went to his bedside to hear his confession and ask if he had debts, what material had been entrusted to him, where he kept his armour and other military gear, how much money, and what plates or jewels he had. After this the sick man was given communion. If the man died, his keys would be handed to the deceased's superior. One set of his bedding remained with the infirmarian while all valuable cloth went to the conventual church and the Hospitaller in overall charge of the infirmaries. Such evidence makes it clear that, from the 14th century onwards, life in the Order of Hospitallers was hardly one of real poverty.

The Crusader Kingdom of Jerusalem suffered a massive defeat at the battle of Gaza in 1239, which finally broke the power of the Crusader States. This shocking setback at the hands of the neighbouring Muslims was symbolized in this 13th-century manuscript by an English chronicler and artist, with the upturned banners of the Hospitallers and Templars flanking the similarly upturned heraldic shields of the defeated crusader leaders. (Historia Anglorum, f.130v, MS. Roy. 14.CVII, British Library, London, England)

Medieval surgical tools, found in various parts of Syria. Though most of these objects are clearly of Islamic or even earlier origin, surgeons employed by the Hospitallers both in the Middle East and within Europe would have used virtually identical tools. (Maristan Nuriya Medical Museum, Damascus, Syria; David Nicolle)

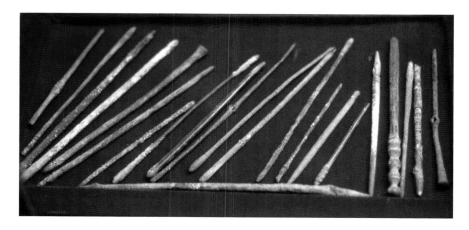

Hospitals dealt with war casualties as well as the sick, and it seems that Hospitaller brethren received the same attention as other Christian casualties. Muslim or other enemy wounded were normally killed. Initially it was the role of surgeons to look after the injured. Surgeons were regarded as *practici* or practical men, unlike the physicians who were *theorici* and thus of higher status. The latter dealt with diet, herbal medicines and the analysis of a patient's urine. Surgeons operated first-aid stations near a scene of combat. In Palestine, wounded men were then brought back to Jerusalem, on the Hospitaller knights' own horses if nothing else was available. In the hospital they were treated by physicians, surgeons and blood-letters – the latter being at the bottom of the medical pecking order.

The doctors and servants or nurses of such hospitals were not themselves members of the Hospitaller Order. Consequently, the Old French Rule provided detailed guidance on how to hire and pay professionals, while Hospitaller statutes of 1182 stated that the hospital required four doctors capable of examining urine, diagnosing diseases and prescribing medicines. Jerusalem became a renowned medical centre some years before it fell to Saladin in 1187, with physicians coming from both Europe and the Middle East to work there. They included Christians, Jews and Muslims, each group perhaps swearing a different oath when contracted. Many Christians disapproved of employing non-Christian doctors or of using advanced Middle Eastern medical knowledge, and there was clear rivalry between physicians of different faiths. But whatever their background, physicians and surgeons who wanted to practise in the Crusader States had to pass a verbal examination conducted by the best doctors in the area.

Less is known about those who could be described as nurses. Again according to the Old French Rule, there were 12 sergeants to each ward in Jerusalem, their duties being to make the beds, keep them clean and to help the sick or injured to the privy or toilet. Two brethren were similarly on duty each night. Sisters of the

Hospitaller Order may have helped tend the sick in the early days, but in later years Hospitaller sisters led an enclosed contemplative form of life. Similarly, although the Hospitallers had female slaves they do not seem to have been employed in the hospital. Those women who did work there and looked after female patients were probably paid servants of the Order. Female patients were found in Hospitaller hospitals, even being mentioned in the very early Anglo-Norman version of the Rule written between 1140 and 1160. Here it was specified that new-born babies should sleep in cots separate from their mothers.

The idea that men who fell in battle during the First Crusade did so as martyrs was a new concept that was not found in the early preaching of the Crusade. The primary justification for the Military Orders was to protect Church and Faith. It was originally defensive rather than offensive and there often seems to have been more focus on the brethren suffering themselves rather than on killing their foes. By the mid-12th century, however, those who fell were clearly regarded as martyrs.

During the 14th and 15th centuries the Hospitallers of Rhodes cultivated a mystique of martyrdom, well illustrated in a speech by the Papal Legate before the Hospitallers and other crusaders sacked Alexandria in 1365. 'Chosen Knights of Christ,' he proclaimed, 'be comforted in the Lord and his Holy Cross. Fight manfully in God's war, fearing not your enemy and hoping for victory from God, for today the gates of Paradise are open.'

The Muristan or 'old hospital' in the Old City of Jerusalem was massively restored in the late 19th century, but still includes substantial architectural fragments from what had been the late 12th-century Hospitaller hospital. (in situ, Muristan, Jerusalem, Israel; Kate Raphael)

Given the Hospitallers' apparent fanaticism, it is hardly surprising that the fall of one of their leaders was a cause for celebration amongst the neighbouring Muslims. One example was the death of the Hospitaller castellan of Crac des Chevaliers in 1170, which led to great rejoicing, according to Ibn al-Athir, a contemporary Muslim historian, because he was 'a man who, through his bravery, occupied an eminent position and who was like a bone stuck in the throat of the Muslims'. The same celebration was seen upon the death of the Hospitaller Master Roger of Moulins in 1187. Saladin offered fifty dinars for every Hospitaller and Templar captive brought to him after the battle of Hattin that year. Also according to Ibn al-Athir, in 1188 it was customary for Saladin to execute all captured brethren of the Military Orders 'because of the violent hatred they bore against the Muslims and because of their bravery'. The eagerness with which the cross on top of the Hospitallers' main church in Jerusalem was pulled down and dragged through the streets when the city fell to Saladin in 1187 similarly reflected the loathing in which the Military Orders were held.

Al-Harawi's book of military advice written for Saladin's immediate successors suggested that the sultan 'should beware of the warrior monks... for he cannot achieve his goals through them, for they have greater fervour in religion, paying no attention to the things of this world. He cannot prevent them from interfering in political affairs. I have investigated them extensively and have found nothing which contradicts this.' In direct contrast to his assessment of the Military Orders, al-Harawi maintained that ordinary Christian churchmen could easily be bribed and made use of.

For the religiously motivated brethren of the Order of Hospitallers, capture may have been more terrifying than death. At the start of the crusades, prisoners were only rarely taken and even in Western Europe systems for ransoming captives were not yet well developed. Even the idea of being taken captive by the 'infidels' does not seem to have been considered and was seen as shameful for men if not for women. Nevertheless, the crusaders soon had to accept the principle of ransoming and negotiation with their Muslim foes during the 12th century. Highly structured, widely recognized and indeed bureaucratic methods of dealing with captivity, ransom and prisoner exchange had existed in both the Islamic and Byzantine Middle East for centuries. For their part, however, the Crusader States learned to prefer ransom money over prisoner exchanges, though they did adopt the Islamic principle of a truce during which military prisoners were swapped. As yet it still appeared to be the responsibility of a captured knight himself and of his family to assemble and pay a ransom, and only in the later 12th century did broader financial structures evolve on the crusader side of the frontier. This period also saw the appearance of specialized religious orders for the redemption of captives, though they developed in the Iberian peninsula before the Middle East.

The Military Orders were amongst those organizations that soon found themselves involved in such matters, often negotiating safe conduct for themselves after surrendering a stronghold to the Muslims. The Military Orders similarly had large numbers of prisoners and slaves in the Middle East, some captured by the Orders, others bought in slave markets by the Order or its vassals, or handed over as the Order's share of booty. However, these unfortunates were not used for prisoner exchange but were kept either to work or for their ransom value.

Those brethren who were taken prisoner often remained incarcerated for a long time, while escapes were rare. In many cases, Islamic rulers were reluctant to release them even for substantial ransoms but preferred to keep such valuable prisoners as diplomatic pawns. The Mamluk Sultanate inherited existing Islamic systems of prisoner exchange and may have developed them further, exchanging prisoners of 'equal value' with the crusaders. The grades in question were those of knight, *barkil*, (which might have meant turcopole or crossbowman), infantryman and peasant. However, in 1263 both the Hospitallers and the Templars refused an exchange with the Mamluk Sultan Baybars because these Military Orders wanted to keep their prisoners as slave labour, constructing new fortifications.

The payment of ransoms for captured Hospitallers and Templars increased during the second half of the 13th century, the Order of Hospitallers being particularly unwilling to let their brethren remain captive for a long time without significant efforts to obtain their release. Yet when a senior man was captured his post tended not to be filled for many years. Meanwhile the difficulty of raising

The village of Temple Balsall in the English Midlands was, as its name suggests, once held by the Military Order of Templars. When they were disbanded early in the 14th century, this property, like so many others across Europe, was transferred to the Hospitallers. They then rebuilt the parish church which is still decorated with weather-worn sculptures, including the examples shown here, which flank the now closed southern door. (David Nicolle)

The Hospitallers acquired estates across much of the Crusader States, including the Kingdom of Jerusalem. The site of the now abandoned Palestinian village of Buqai'ah, known to the crusaders as Bugaea, near the similarly abandoned al-Majami bridge over the river Jordan, was one such frontier estate. (David Nicolle)

ransoms was illustrated by the fate of an English Hospitaller, Roger of Stanegrave, who was captured in the Holy Land and was still a prisoner-of-war in 1318, 27 years after the fall of Acre when he seems to have been taken captive. He was reportedly still trying to assemble a ransom of 12,000 gold florins from friends and family. The records seem to show that prisoners from the Military Orders had less chance of liberation in the Middle East than if they had been captured on the Iberian front. Special arrangements could be made for men of certain nationalities. Thus Catalan Hospitallers and Templars captured at the fall of Acre were released, though only after spending 15 years in Mamluk jails. They included brothers Lope de Linares and Guillem de Villalba, along with ten squires and servants of assorted nationalities.

Soon there were references not only to prisoners but also to renegades, one of the towers of Sidon proving to be defended by Provençal renegades when it was taken by the crusaders in 1108. Given the large numbers of prisoners-of-war on both sides during the 12th century, often running into tens of thousands, it is not surprising that some turned renegade. There seem, however, to have been more examples of Templars doing so than Hospitallers. Similarly, there were plenty of references to Templars rather than Hospitallers being held captive in the Middle East during the decades before the catastrophe at Hattin. Neither are there reports of any known Hospitaller renegades holding senior positions in Islamic armies, although a Spanish ex-Templar commanded the forces of Damascus for the Ayyubid ruler al-Nasir in 1229. In complete contrast, the Christian Patriarch of Alexandria claimed that there were 10,000 Christian

renegades in Islamic service only three years earlier, but without identifying them any further. In 1402, when the Venetian traveller Emmanuel Piloti visited Egypt, he reported that some 200 French and Italian captives had converted to Islam and had risen to prominence within the Mamluk military system. They apparently formed part of the Cairo Citadel garrison, but were not known to have included any ex-Hospitallers.

Muslim treatment of captured crusaders tended to be milder in times of success and harsher in times of defeat. Occasionally it seems as if the execution of certain categories of crusader captives was regarded as a religious duty, though records also mention individuals refusing to take part in such killing while accepting its legal validity. As was also the case in Europe, higher-ranking individuals were more likely to be ransomed than those of lower status. In contrast, captives of obvious military significance could find themselves forming part of a victory parade. There were, for example, many cases of captured 'knights' being sent for such purposes to cities as far away as Baghdad or Cairo, often with their complete military equipment.

A wall-painting by Giulio Romano, made around 1525 in what are now called the Raphael Rooms in the Vatican Palace of Rome, shows Hospitaller knight brethren serving as papal guards during a conclave of cardinals. (2006 Alinari/TopFoto)

The castle of Crac des Chevaliers was badly damaged when the Mamluks finally took it from the Hospitaller garrison. However, this damage was largely confined to the southern and eastern side. The series of box-machicolations seen here is in the southern part of the western wall and dates from the Hospitaller period. (David Nicolle)

In addition to facing death from disease, in battle, or during prolonged imprisonment, Hospitaller brethren might be sent on hazardous diplomatic missions. This happened shortly before the final Mamluk attack upon Acre. Sultan Qala'un had prepared the campaign but his sudden death led to it being postponed, so the crusader authorities tried to take advantage of this delay and sent an embassy to Cairo. It was led by the Arabic specialist Philip Mainboeuf, a Templar knight named Bartholomew Pizan and a Hospitaller secretary named George. Unfortunately, the new Sultan al-Ashraf refused to see them and they were instead thrown into prison, where they died under unknown circumstances.

Those who fell in battle in defeat often seem to have been left for the carrion birds or animals. Almost nothing is known about those who fell in victory, though they would certainly have been given a decent Christian burial. On the other hand, very elaborate regulations governed the burial of Hospitaller brethren, at least those who died within their convents, and these were followed by services of remembrance. During the late 12th century, for example, the bodies were laid out before burial for a length of time that depended upon what hour of day they died. The body was then placed on a bier draped with a flag of the Order, surrounded by candles and watched over within the church while clerks intoned psalms. All the brothers of the man's convent attended the burial unless they had been ordered elsewhere. This burial process seems to have remained unchanged for the following centuries, though from 1278 all brothers were buried in their mantles.

The anniversaries of the deaths of Hospitaller brethren were commemorated each year and were listed in the calendar. The Order's Rule stipulated that 30 masses were to be read for each dead brother, while clerical brethren or other

Silifke castle on the southern coast of Anatolia, now Turkey, was the Hospitallers' most important mainland possession in the Middle East outside the Crusader States. It was given to the Order by the Armenian Kingdom of Cilicia to defend the western entrance to the fertile Cilician coastal plain and was held from 1210 until 1226. (David Nicolle)

clerks recited psalms and the lay brethren said 150 paternosters every evening for the souls of the Order's benefactors. From 1262 onwards, Vespers and vigils for the dead were also sung every Sunday before Lent, while on the first Sunday in Lent itself there was a solemn requiem office for the souls of deceased Masters and brethren. In other respects all the deceased brethren were treated equally, and only two members of the Order of Hospitallers were canonized during this period. Both were Italians, St Ubaldesca of Pisa who died in 1206 and St Hugh of Genoa who died in 1230. They were both canonized for their charitable Christian lives rather than for military reasons.

The burial of dead pilgrims as well as dead brothers had been an important duty for the Hospitallers in Acre and there were also ceremonies in other centres. When the crusader knight Geoffrey de Joinville died at Crac des Chevaliers in 1203 or 1204 he was buried in the Hospitaller castle's chapel, where his shield also hung until it was taken back to Joinville in France by the famous crusader and chronicler Jean de Joinville in the early 1250s. Unfortunately this shield was stolen from Joinville church by invading German troops in 1544.

Epilogue: Later History and Legacy

After the fall of Rhodes, King Charles V of Spain became the Hospitallers' most important patron and offered the Order the island of Malta and the somewhat vulnerable Spanish-ruled port of Tripoli in Libya. The French, who were at that time bitter rivals of Spain, resisted this handover because they feared the Hospitallers would now become a mere addition to Spanish military power. Nor were the Hospitallers wholly enthusiastic and in fact the Order sent commissioners to look at alternative locations, including Minorca and Ibiza off the Spanish coast as well as Ischia off the Italian coast. Unfortunately none were made available by their current rulers, so the Hospitallers had little choice but to accept King Charles V's offer.

The Order eventually moved to Malta in 1530. Their commissioners had not reported very favourably on the island. Wood was apparently so scarce that it was sold by weight, while cow-dung and thistles were commonly used as fuel. Many of the houses in the crumbling main town of Mdina, known in Italian as Città Notabile, were uninhabited. Even the small coastal castle of Sant Angelo only had three cannon and a few mortars, though it did overlook the great harbour of Birgu (Il Borgo), which was considered the third best in the central Mediterranean after those of Syracuse in Sicily and Taranto in southern Italy. Furthermore, Malta did not command any important shipping lane and so its strategic value seemed rather small.

The population of Malta consisted of about 12,000 Arabic-speaking peasants under a local aristocracy that claimed descent from Norman, Italian and Catalan conquerors. The Maltese nobility were themselves not keen on their island being handed over to the overbearing Hospitaller brethren, but they were in no position to do anything about it.

One of the few positive aspects of Malta was that it had developed into a major centre of cotton production. The island's Muslim Arab rulers had introduced

OPPOSITE

Once again Italian art provides the most detailed and accurate representation of naval matters in the medieval Mediterranean. In this episode from the life of St Nicholas, painted by Ambroglio Lorenzetti around 1332, large ships are anchored while their cargoes and passengers are taken ashore in smaller boats. Such scenes could have been commonplace around the Hospitallers' island possessions in the Aegean. Note that one ship even uses a wooden chute, apparently for grain that is poured into a shallow draught barge. (Uffizi Gallery, Florence, Italy/The Bridgeman Art Library)

An archway leading to the inner courtyard of the Hospitaller castle of Belvoir, overlooking the Jordan valley in Palestine. This remarkable fortress is usually seen as the first true example of a concentric castle surrounded by a sequence of defences. On the other hand, this layout might merely reflect the fact that it was designed as a monastic convent for the Hospitaller brethen, as well as being a castle. (David Nicolle)

cotton in the early medieval period, and it could be used to make ships' sails. The islands also produced the spice cumin, which was a high-value export crop. Some wheat and grapes were also grown but even without the presence of Hospitaller brethren and all their servants, Malta still had to import food.

The Hospitallers were, however, permitted to import wheat from Sicily free of export duty, and in return for its new home, the Order agreed to pay an annual 'rent' of one hawk or gerfalcon each year to the king of Spain.

During the early years of Hospitaller rule, the harbour town of Birgu expanded slowly and, after the defeat of the great Ottoman siege of 1565, its name was changed to Valletta in honour of the Hospitallers' courageous Master, Jean Parisot de la Valette. The events of 1565 have sometimes been described as a turning point in European history but in reality they neither halted Ottoman expansion elsewhere, nor even seriously damaged the Ottoman Turks' rising naval power. Perhaps as a result, the Hospitaller convent could not be said to have fully settled into its new Maltese home until the later 16th century.

By then the Order of Hospitallers had suffered many serious blows elsewhere. Its properties in England and Scandinavia were lost as a result of the Protestant Reformation and the English langue ceased to exist except in name. Elsewhere many commanderies had been raided by revolutionary Anabaptists and even within Catholic Savoy and Portugal some properties were confiscated by local rulers. Within Germany the situation was even more complicated. Here several powerful princes, including the Margrave of Brandenburg, became Protestant and consequently confiscated the Catholic Order's properties. In some places there were even cases of brethren having to pay the salaries of Protestant pastors. A few of the Order's own priests converted to Lutheranism and for a while the number of German brother-knights fell from 40 to 26. In 1551 the Order declared the brethren in Brandenburg in north-eastern Germany to be 'rebels', but many other German members of the Order urged a peaceful solution to these internal quarrels, which was finally achieved at the end of the 16th century.

While the Hospitallers established themselves on Malta and the neighbouring island of Gozo, they gradually lost most of their territorial possessions on the European mainland, even in those areas that remained Catholic. Eventually they were reduced to owning just the priories of Bohemia and Messina, finally losing the latter in 1860.

Napoleon seized Malta itself in 1798 and it was not until just over 35 years later that the Order's headquarters was firmly re-established in Rome. In 1879 the Pope recognized the re-creation of the post of Grand Master of the Hospitallers, his function having been carried out by lieutenants of the Mastership for almost a century. Despite this diminution of status, the Hospitallers continued to be regarded as a sovereign entity, with diplomatic representatives in several world capitals, their own diplomatic service and even the authority to issue passports.

THE HOSPITALLERS TODAY

Two parts of the Order of Hospitallers survive in a Protestant form, neither of which is recognized by the Pope or by the head of the original Roman Catholic order. One is the Bailliwick of Brandenburg, which was re-established by the King of Prussia in 1852 and supports several hospitals in Germany. The other is the English Grand Priory, which was re-established in 1831 and was authorized by a British royal charter in 1888. Today the monarch is its sovereign head, while the organization also controls the St John Ambulance Brigade and Association, plus an eye hospital in Jerusalem. The four non-Catholic Orders of St John in Germany, Sweden, the Netherlands and the United Kingdom together form an alliance.

Appendices

Appendix I

MASTERS OF THE ORDER OF HOSPITALLERS OF ST JOHN

1113	Blessed Gerard becomes first Master of the Order
1120	Death of the Blessed Gerard; the Blessed Raymond du Puy becomes Master of the Order
1160	Auger de Balben
1162	Arnold de Comps becomes Master of the Order, followed by Gilbert d'Assailly the same year
1170	Cast de Murols
1172	Jobert de Syrie
1177	Roger de Moulins
1187	Armengaud d'Asp
1190	Garnier de Naples
1193	Geoffrey de Donjon
1203	Alfonso de Portugal
1206	Geoffrey le Rat
1207	Garin de Montaigu
1228	Bertrand de Thessy
1230	Guerin (rest of name unknown)
1236	Bertrand de Comps
1239	Pierre de Vieille Bride
1242	Guillaume de Châteauneuf
1258	Hugh Revel
1277	Nicholas Lorgne
1285	Jean de Villiers
1293	Eudes des Pins

This stylized portrait of the Hospitaller Grand Master Juan Fernandez de Heredia fills a decorated initial in a late 14th-century Spanish manuscript. (Archivo Iconografico, S.A./Corbis)

1296   Guillaume de Villaret

1305   Foulques de Villaret

1317   Foulques de Villaret is deposed; Gerard de Pins becomes temporary Lieutenant of the Order

1319   Hélion de Villeneuve

1346   Dieudonné de Gozon

1353   Pierre de Corneillan

1355   Roger de Pins

1365   Raimond Bèrenger

1374   Robert de Juilly

1377   Juan Fernandez de Heredia

1383   Riccardo Caracciolo appointed by Pope Urban VI as Master but not acknowledged in Rhodes (thereafter referred to as 'anti-Master')

1395   Riccardo Caracciolo resigns

1396   Philibert de Naillac

1421	Antonio de Fluvia
1437	Jean de Lastic
1454	Jacques de Milly
1461	Raimundo Zacosta
1467	Giovanni Battista Orsini
1476	Pierre d'Aubusson
1503	Emery d'Amboise
1512	Guy de Blanchefort
1513	Fabrizio del Carretto
1521	Philippe Villiers de l'Isle Adam
1534	Pietrino del Ponte
1535	Didier de Tholon Sainte-Jalle
1536	Juan de Homedes y Coscon
1553	Claude de la Sengle
1557	Jean Parisot de la Valette
1568	Death of Jean Parisot de la Valette

Appendix 2

RELICS OF A WARLIKE PAST

DOCUMENTS

As one of the largest, richest and most powerful trans-national organizations in the medieval world, the Order of St John of the Hospital of Jerusalem left a huge amount of documents, often with elaborate seals. These are preserved in archives throughout Europe, though mostly in Rome, while examples of Hospitaller seals can be found in many museums. In addition to its own small museum, the Museum of the Order of St John in London has an excellent library which contains the famous Rhodes Missal as well as other valuable written sources.

ARMS AND ARMOUR

A considerable amount of arms and armour associated with the Hospitallers survives in various museums, but none of it dates from the 12th or 13th centuries. The armour found at Rhodes in the late 19th or early 20th century has since been dispersed across several museums and collections. Some pieces have even been lost. Most of the armour displayed in the world's museums was made for wealthy princes to show off their splendour, and so ranks as art as much as armour. In contrast, the Rhodes armour is particularly important because it is ordinary military kit. The collection seems to have been the remains of an arsenal that was probably tipped into a corner by the Ottoman Turks after they captured Rhodes

The breast- and back-plates of the armour belonging to the Hospitaller Grand Master Jean Parisot de la Valette. He is said to have worn it during the great Ottoman siege of Malta in 1565. The armour itself is of Italian manufacture and style. (Armoury of the Knights of St John. Malta; G.F. Laking)

in 1522 because such matériel was not used by Ottoman soldiers. There are no weapons in the Rhodes collection because these would have been acceptable to the victors.

Precisely where the pieces were found is unclear, and it is possible that they may have been used for a while by local guards following the fall of Hospitaller Rhodes. Nor is it certain when these pieces of armour were brought back to Western Europe. Pilfering may have started as early as the mid-19th century, and pieces were still turning up in the 1920s. The largest number of items was actually manufactured in northern Italy, while others were made in Germany, Flanders, France, England and Iberia, though such identification is on the basis of style only as few of the objects have identifiable armourer's marks.

The famous Armoury of the Knights at Valletta in Malta has another superb collection of arms and armour, but almost all dates from a later period. Only a few items come from the time of the Great Siege in 1565.

Appendix 3

HOSPITALLER BUILDINGS

The Middle East and various parts of Europe are dotted with castles that were either built by, or were at one time garrisoned by, the Hospitallers. Those in the Middle and Near East are listed below. Europe has an even larger number of both churches and secular, non-military structures once owned by the Order. The latter range from commanderies that became manor houses, to hospitals

The northern city wall and citadel of Acre. Recent archaeological excavations have shown that this part of the city's existing fortifications is built upon those dating from the crusader occupation if not earlier. The upper parts, of course, were rebuilt many centuries later, including the citadel that stands on top of the medieval Hospitaller convent. (David Nicolle)

and even barns. Of all the locations associated with the Order of Hospitallers following their expulsion from the Holy Land, nothing compares with Rhodes and the neighbouring islands, unless it is Malta, where almost all the surviving Hospitaller architecture dates from a later period.

THE MAIN CASTLES

Cyprus
> Kolossi: castle and sugar refinery
> Paphos: excavations of uncompleted castle

Greece
> Kálymnos: Pothía, castle; Khorió, castle
> Kastellórizo: castle
> Kos: Kos town, castle; Old Pylai, castle; Andimákhia, castle
> Léros: Plátanos, castle
> Nísíros: castle
> Rhodes: fortified city of Rhodes enclosing many other Hospitaller buildings;
> > Lindos, castle; Phileremos, restored Hospitaller church; Arkhangelos, castle;
> > Pharaklos, castle; Alimnia, castle; Kastéllos, castle; Monolithos, castle
> Simi: Khorió, castle
> Tílos: several castles, of which Megálo Khorió is the biggest

Israel

Arsuf: excavations of ruined castle and town
Ascalon: excavated ruins of city wall
Bayt Jibrin: ruins of fortification
Belvoir: extensive excavated ruins
Mount Tabor: ruined fortifications
Qalansuma: ruins of fortified tower

Lebanon

Akkar: ruins of extensive castle

Syria

Jableh: some remains of fortified town
Crac des Chevaliers: huge, almost complete castle
Marqab: huge, almost complete castle
Qala'at Banu Israil: ruined castle
Qala'at Yahmur: almost complete small castle

Turkey

Bodrum: castle
Silifke: huge, almost complete castle
Toprak-kale: huge, almost complete castle.

All that remains of the once lofty citadel of Arsuf are its foundations. This coastal town was held by the Hospitallers until it fell to the Mamluks in 1265. (David Nicolle)

Bibliography

Alliott, E. A., *The Rhodes Missal* (London, 1980).

Anon., *The Maritime Siege of Malta 1565: National Maritime Museum* (London).

Atiya, A. S., *The Crusade of Nicopolis* (London, 1934).

Azzopardi, J. (ed.), *The Sovereign Military Order of St John of Jerusalem, of Rhodes and Malta: The Order's Early Legacy* (Valletta, 1989).

Balard, M., 'I possedimenti degli Ospidalieri nella Terrasanta (secoli XII–XIII)', in J. C. Restagno (ed.), *Cavalieri di San Giovanni e Territorio* (Borgighera, 1999), 473–505.

Barquero Goñi, C., 'El caracter militar de la Orden de San Juan en Castilla y Leon (siglos XII–XIV)', *Revista de Historia Militar*, 73 (1992), 53–80.

Biller, T., 'Der Crac des Chevaliers – neue Forschungen', *Chateau Gaillard*, 20 (2002), 51–55.

Bonet Donato, M., *La Orden del Hospital en la Corona de Aragon, poder y gobierno en la Castellania de Amposta (ss. XII–XV)* (Madrid, 1994).

Borchardt, K., 'The Hospitallers, Bohemia and the Empire 1250–1330', in J. Sarnowsky (ed.), *Mendicants, Military Orders and Regionalism in Medieval Europe* (Aldershot, 1999), 201–231.

Borchardt, K., 'The Hospitallers in Pomerania: Between the Priories of Bohemia and Alamania,', in H. J. Nicholson (ed.), *The Military Orders, Volume 2: Welfare and Warfare* (Aldershot, 1998), 295–306.

Borchardt, K. (et al. eds.), *The Hospitallers, the Mediterranean and Europe: Festschrift for Anthony Luttrell* (Aldershot, 2007).

Bracewell, C. W., 'Corsairs and the Holy War in the Early Modern Mediterranean', *St John Historical Society Proceedings*, 4 (1992), 33–39.

Brundage, J. A., 'The Lawyers of the Military Orders', in M. Barber (ed.), *The Military Orders: Fighting for the Faith and Caring for the Sick* (Aldershot, 1994), 346–357.

Burgtorf, J., 'The Order of the Hospital's High Dignitaries and their Claims on the Inheritance of Deceased Brethren – Regulations and Conflicts', in M. Balard (ed.), *Autour de la Première Croisade* (Paris, 1996), 255–265.

Burgtorf, J., 'Wind beneath the Wings: Subordinate Headquarters Officials in the

Hospital', in H. J. Nicholson (ed.), *The Military Orders, Volume 2: Welfare and Warfare* (Aldershot, 1998), 217–224.

Burgtorf, J. and Nicholson, H., *International Mobility in the Military Orders (Twelfth to Fifteenth Centuries): Travelling on Christ's Business* (Cardiff, 2006).

Butler, L., *The Siege of Rhodes 1480* (London).

Cagnin, G., *Templari e Giovanniti in Territorio Trevigiano (secoli XII–XIV)* (Treviso, 1992).

Carraz, D., 'Moine soldat; un nouvel idéal', and 'Des Ordres attirés par la ville' (mostly dealing with the Military Orders in Provence), *Histoire et Images Médiévales*, 13 (Apr–May 2007), 36–53.

Cathcart King, D. J., 'The Taking of Le Krak des Chevaliers in 1271', *Antiquity*, 23 (1949), 83–92.

Caucci von Saucken, P. G., 'Gli Ordini Militari e Ospidalieri sul Camino de Santiago', in E. Coli (et al. eds.), *Militia sacra: gli Ordini Militari tra Europe e Terrasanta* (Perugia, 1994), 85–100.

Cohen, M., 'The Fortification of the Fortress of Gybelin', in N. Faucherre (et al. eds.), *La fortification au temps des Croisades* (Rennes, 2004), 67–75.

Coli, E., (et al. eds.), *Militia sacra: gli Ordini Militari tra Europe e Terrasanta* (Perugia, 1994).

D'Agostino, L., 'Les Moines-Soldats en Auvergne et Velay', *Histoire et Images Médiévales*, 13 (Apr–May 2007), 54–63.

De Ayala Martinez, C., *Libro de privilegios de la Orden de San Juan de Jerusalem en Castille y Leon, Siglos XII–XV* (Madrid, 1995).

Delaville le Roulx, J. M. A., *Les archives, la bibliothèque et le trésor de l'Ordre de Saint Jean de Jérusalem* (Paris, 1883).

Delaville le Roulx, J. M. A. (ed.), *Cartulaire générale de l'Ordre des Hospitaliers de St Jean de Jérusalem* (Paris, 1894–1906).

Delaville le Roulx, J. M. A., *Les Hospitaliers à Rhodes (1310–1421)* (Paris, 1913; repr. London, 1974).

Delaville le Roulx, J .M. A., *Les Hospitaliers en Terre Sainte et à Chypre 1100–1310* (Paris, 1904).

Deschamps, P., *Les Chateaux des Croises en Terre Sainte: le Crac des Chevaliers* (Paris 1934).

Edgington, S., 'Administrative Regulations for the Hospital of St John in Jerusalem dating from the 1180s', *Crusades*, 4 (2005), 21–38.

Edgington, S., 'The Hospital of St John in Jerusalem', in Z. Amar (et al. eds.), *Medicine in Jerusalem throughout the Ages* (Jerusalem, 1997), 9–25.

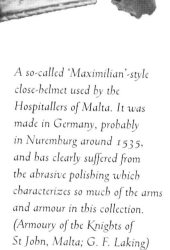

A so-called 'Maximilian'-style close-helmet used by the Hospitallers of Malta. It was made in Germany, probably in Nuremburg around 1535, and has clearly suffered from the abrasive polishing which characterizes so much of the arms and armour in this collection. (Armoury of the Knights of St John, Malta; G. F. Laking)

Edgington, S., 'Medical Care in the Hospital of St John in Jerusalem', in H. J. Nicholson (ed.), *The Military Orders, Volume 2: Welfare and Warfare* (Aldershot, 1998) 27–33.

Favreau-Lilie. M.-L., 'The Military Orders and the Escape of the Christian Population from the Holy Land in 1291', *Journal of Medieval History*, 19 (1993), 201–227.

Folda, J., 'Crusader Frescoes at Crac des Chevaliers and Marqab Castles', *Dumbarton Oaks Papers*, 36 (1982), 177–210.

Forey, A. J., 'Literacy and Learning in the Military Orders during the C12th & C13th', in H. J. Nicholson (ed.), *The Military Orders, Volume 2: Welfare and Warfare* (Aldershot, 1998), 185–206.

Forey, A. J., 'The Militarization of the Hospital of St John', *Studia Monastica*, 26 (1984), 75–89.

Forey, A. J., *Military Orders and Crusaders* (London, 1994).

Forey, A. J., 'The Military Orders and the Holy War against Christians in the Thirteenth Century', *English Historical Review*, 104 (1989), 1–24.

Forey, A. J., 'The Military Orders and the Spanish Reconquest in the Twelfth and Thirteenth Centuries', *Traditio*, 40 (1984), 197–234.

Forey, A. J., *The Military Orders from the Twelfth to the Early Fourteenth Centuries* (London, 1991).

Forey, A. J., 'Novitiate and Instruction in the Military Orders during the Twelfth and Thirteenth Centuries', *Speculum*, 61 (1986), 1–17.

Forey, A. J., 'Recruitment to the Military Orders (Twelfth to Mid-Fourteenth Centuries)', *Viator*, 17 (1986), 139–171.

Forey, A. J., 'Women and the Military Orders in the Twelfth and Thirteenth Centuries', *Studia Monastica*, 29 (1987), 63–129.

Gervers, M., 'Pro defensione Terre Sanctae: The Development and Exploitation of the Hospitallers' Landed Estate in Essex', in M. Barber (ed.), *The Military Orders: Fighting for the Faith and Caring for the Sick* (Aldershot, 1994), 3–20.

Goldmann, Z., *Akko in the Time of the Crusades: The Convent of the Order of St John* (Jerusalem, 1994).

Goldmann, Z., 'The Hospice of the Knights of St John in Akko', *Archaeology*, 29 (1966), 182–189.

Gooder, E., *Temple Balsall: From Hospitallers to a Caring Community, 1322 to Modern Times* (Chichester, 1999).

Harot, E., *Essai d'Armorial des Grands Maîtres de l'Ordre de St Jean à Jérusalem* (Rome, 1911).

Henry, M., *Les Ordres Militaires en Lorraine* (Metz, 2006).

Heutger, N., 'Die Ritterorden im Heiligen Land: Die Hospitaler und Ordensgemeinschaften', in H.-J. Kotzur (ed.), *Kein Krieg ist Heilig: Die Kreuz-Zuge* (Mainz, 2004), 137–153.

Hiestand, R., 'Ein unbekanntes Privileg Furst Bohemonds II von Antiochia fur das Hospital von Marz 1127', *Archiv fur Diplomatik*, 43 (1998), 27–46.

Hunyadi, Z., 'The Hospitallers in the Kingdom of Hungary: Commanderies, Personnel, and a Particular Activity up to c.1400', in Z. Hunyadi and J. Laszlovszky (eds.), *The Crusades and the Military Orders: Expanding the Frontiers of Medieval Latin Christianity* (Budapest, 2001), 253–268.

Hunyadi, Z., 'The Hungarian Nobility and the Knights of St John', in N. Coulet and J.-M. Matz (eds), *La noblesse dans les territoires angevins à la fin du Moyen Age* (Ecole Française de Rome, Rome, 2000), 607–618.

Josserand, P., 'La figure du commandeur dans les prieurés castillans et léonais du Temple et de l'Hôpital: une approche prosopographique (fin XIIe–milieu XIVe siècle)', in *Ordens Militares: guerra, religião, poder e cultura – Actas do III Encontro sobre Ordens Militares*, vol. 1 (Lisbon, 1999), 149–178.

Karassava-Tsilingiri, F., 'The Fifteenth Century Hospital of Rhodes: Tradition and Innovation', in M. Barber (ed.), *The Military Orders: Fighting for the Faith and Caring for the Sick* (Aldershot, 1994), 89–96.

Karassava-Tsilingri, F., 'Fifteenth Century Hospitaller Architecture on Rhodes: Patrons and Master Builders', in H. J. Nicholson (ed.), *The Military Orders, Volume 2. Welfare and Warfare* (Aldershot, 1998), 259–266.

Karcheski, W. J., and Richardson, T., *The Medieval Armour from Rhodes* (Leeds, 2000).

Kedar, B., 'A C12th description of the Jerusalem Hospital', in H. J. Nicholson (ed.), *The Military Orders, Volume 2: Welfare and Warfare* (Aldershot, 1998), 3–26.

Kedar, B. Z., and Schein, S., 'Un projet de "passage particulier" proposé par l'Ordre de l'Hôpital, 1306–1307', *Bibliothèque de l'Ecole de Chartres*, 137 (1979), 211–226.

King, E. J., *The Knights Hospitallers in the Holy Land* (London, 1931).

King, E. J., *The Rules, Statutes and Customs of the Hospitallers 1099–1310* (London, 1934).

Kucznski, S. K. (ed.), *Zakon Maltanski w Polsce (Order of St John in Poland)* (Warsaw, 2000).

Laking, G. F., *A Catalogue of the Armour and Arms in the Armoury of the Knights of St John of Jerusalem now in the Palace, Valletta, Malta* (London).

Legras, A.-M., 'Une source priviligiée de l'histoire de l'hôpital en Occident au XIVe siècle: L'enquête Pontificale de 1373', in E. Coli (ed.), *Militia sacra: gli Ordini Militari tra Europa e Terrasanta* (Perugia, 1994), 49–53.

Libor, J. and Jesensky, V., 'Hospitaller and Templar Commanderies in Bohemia and Moravia; Their Structure and Architectural Forms', in H. J. Nicholson (ed.), *The Military Orders, Volume 2: Welfare and Warfare* (Aldershot, 1998), 235–249.

Licence, T., 'The Templars and the Hospitallers, Christ and the Saints', *Crusades*, 4 (2005), 39–58.

Ligato, G., 'Il Magister Ospidaliero Ruggero des Moulins nella crisi finale del Regno Latino di Gerusalemme (1182–1187)', *Antoniarum*, 71 (1996), 495–522.

Lock, P., 'The Military Orders in Mainland Greece', in M. Barber (ed.), *The Military Orders: Fighting for the Faith and Caring for the Sick* (Aldershot, 1994), 333–339.

Luttrell, A., 'The Hospitallers' Early Written Records', in E. France (ed.), *The Crusades and their Sources; Essays Presented to Bernard Hamilton* (Aldershot, 1998), 135–154.

Luttrell, A., (ed.), *Latin Greece, the Hospitallers and the Crusades 1291–1440* (Aldershot, 1982).

Luttrell, A., 'An English Contribution to the Hospitaller Castle at Bodrum in Turkey: 1407–1437', in H. J. Nicholson (ed.), *The Military Orders, Volume 2: Welfare and Warfare* (Aldershot, 1998), 163–172.

Luttrell, A., 'El final de la dominacio Catalana d'Atenes: La Companijia Navarresa i els Hospitalers', *L'Avenc*, 213 (April 1997), 30–34.

Luttrell, A., 'Emmanuele Piloti and Criticism of the Knights Hospitallers of Rhodes: 1306–1444', *Annales de l'Ordre Souverain Militaire de Malte*, 20 (1962), 1–20.

Luttrell, A., 'Ermengol de Aspa, Provisor of the Hospital; 1188', *Crusades*, 4 (2005), 15–20.

Luttrell, A., 'Hospitaller Birgu: 1530–1536', *Crusades*, 2 (2003), 121–150.

Luttrell, A., 'Hospitaller Life in Aragon, 1319–1370', in D. W. Lomax and D. Mackenzie (eds.), *God and Man in Medieval Spain: Essays in Honour of J. R. L. Highfield* (Warminster, 1989), 97–115.

Luttrell, A., 'Intrigue, Schism and Violence amongst the Hospitallers of Rhodes: 1377–1384', *Speculum*, 61 (1966), 30–48.

Luttrell, A., 'Lindos and the Defence of Rhodes: 1306–1522', *Rivista di Studi Byzantini e Neoellenici*, 22–23 (1985–86), 317–332.

Luttrell, A., 'Malta and Rhodes: Hospitallers and Islanders', in V. Mallia-Milanes (ed.), *Hospitaller Malta 1530–1798* (Malta, 1993), 255–284.

Luttrell, A., 'Rhodes and Jerusalem: 1291–1411', *Byzantinische Forschungen*, 12 (1987), 189–207.

Luttrell, A., 'The Earliest Hospitallers', in B. Z. Kedar (et al. eds.), *Montjoie: Studies in Crusade History in Honour of Hans Eberhard Mayer* (Aldershot, 1997), 37–54.

Luttrell, A., 'The Hospitallers in Cyprus; 1310–1378', in *Acts of the International Congress of Cypriot Studies, I* (Nicosia, 1972), 161–171.

Luttrell, A., 'The Hospitallers in Cyprus after 1291', in *Kypriakai Spoudai* (Nicosia, 1986), 155–184.

Luttrell, A., 'The Hospitallers of Rhodes and the Mausoleum at Halicarnassus', in V. P. Goss (ed.), *The Meeting of Two Worlds, Cultural Exchange between East and West during the Period of the Crusades* (Kalamazoo, 1986), 161–165.

Luttrell, A., 'The Hospitallers of Rhodes Confront the Turks: 1306–1421', in P. F. Gallagher (ed.), *Christians, Jews and other Worlds: Patterns of Conflict and Accommodation* (Lanha, 1988), 80–116.

Luttrell, A., 'The Hospitallers' Historical Activities: 1291–1400', *Annales de l'Ordre Souverein Militaire de Malte*, 24 (1966), 1–10.

Luttrell, A., 'The Hospitallers' Historical Activities: 1400–1530', *Annales de l'Ordre Souverein Militaire de Malte*, 25 (1967), 145–150.

Luttrell, A., 'The Hospitallers' Historical Activities: 1530–1630', *Annales de l'Ordre Souverein Militaire de Malte*, 26 (1968), 57–69.

Luttrell, A., 'The Hospitallers' Interventions in Cilician Armenia: 1291–1375', in T. S. R. Boase (ed.), *The Cilician Kingdom of Armenia* (Edinburgh, 1978), 118–144.

Luttrell, A., 'The Hospitallers' Medical Tradition 1291–1530', in M. Barber (ed.), *The Military Orders: Fighting for the Faith and Caring for the Sick* (Aldershot, 1994), 64–81.

Luttrell, A., 'The Later History of the Mausoleion and its Utilization in the Hospitaller Castle at Bodrum', *Jutland Archaeological Society Publications*, 15 (1986), 114–222.

Luttrell, A., 'The Military and Naval Organization of the Hospitallers at Rhodes, 1310–1444', in Z. H. Nowak (ed.), *Das Kriegswesen der Ritterorden im Mittelalter, Ordines militares – Colloquia Torunensia Historica*, VI (Torun, 1991), 133–153.

Luttrell, A., 'The Order of St John from Acre to Malta', *St John Historical Society Proceedings*, 4 (1992), 1–6.

Luttrell, A., 'Slavery at Rhodes: 1306–1440', *Bulletin de l'Institut historique belge de Rome*, 46–47 (1976–77), 81–100.

Luttrell, A., *The Hospitaller State on Rhodes and its Western Provinces* (1999).

Luttrell, A., *The Hospitallers in Cyprus, Rhodes, Greece and the West (1291–1440)* (London, 1978).

Luttrell, A., *The Town of Rhodes 1306–1356* (Rhodes, 2003).

Mallia-Milanes, V., 'Corsairs Parading Crosses: the Hospitallers and Venice, 1530–1778', in M. Barber (ed.), *The Military Orders: Fighting for the Faith and Caring for the Sick* (Aldershot, 1994), 103–112.

Mallia-Milanes, V. (ed.), *Hospitaller Malta 1530–1798* (Malta, 1993).

Megaw, P., 'A Castle in Cyprus Attributable to the Hospital?', in M. Barber (ed.), *The Military Orders: Fighting for the Faith and Caring for the Sick* (Aldershot, 1994), 42–51.

Menache, S., 'The Hospitallers during Clement V's Pontificate: The Spoiled Sons of the Papacy?', in H. J. Nicholson (ed.), *The Military Orders, Volume 2: Welfare and Warfare* (Aldershot, 1998), 153–162.

Mitchell, P. D., *Surgery in the Crusades: St John Historical Society Proceedings* (1997).

Nicholson, H. J., 'Before William of Tyre: European Reports of the Military Orders' Deeds in the East 1150–85', in Nicholson, H. J. (ed.), *The Military Orders, Volume 2: Welfare and Warfare* (Aldershot, 1998), 111–118.

Nicholson, H. J., 'Jacquemart Gielee's Renart le Nouvel: The Image of the Military Orders on the Eve of the Loss of Acre', in J. Loades (ed.), *Monastic Studies* (Bangor, 1990), 182–189.

Nicholson, H. J., 'Knights and Lovers: The Military Orders in the Romantic Literature of the Thirteenth Century', in M. Barber (ed.), *The Military Orders: Fighting for the Faith and Caring for the Sick* (Aldershot, 1994), 340–345.

Nicholson, H. J., 'The Knights Hospitaller on the Frontiers of the British Isles', in J. Sarnowsky (ed.), *Mendicants, Military Orders and Regionalism in Medieval Europe* (Aldershot, 1999), 47–57.

Nicholson, H. J., *The Military Orders in the Romantic Literature of the C13th: St John Historical Society Proceedings* (1993).

Prawer, J,. 'Military Orders and Crusader Politics in the Second Half of the XIIIth Century', in J. Fleckenstein and M. Hellmannn (eds.), *Die geistlichen Riterorden Europas* (Sigmaringen, 1980), 217–229.

Pringle, R. D., 'Castle Chapels in the Frankish East', in N. Faucherre (et al. eds.), *La fortification au temps des Croisades* (Rennes, 2004,) 25–41.

Rabie, H., 'Mamluk Campaigns against Rhodes (A.D. 1440–1444)', in C. E. Bosworth (ed.), *Essays in Honour of Bernard Lewis: The Islamic World from Classical to Modern Times* (Princeton, 1989), 281–286.

Rees, W., *A History of the Order of St John of Jerusalem in Wales and the Welsh Border* (Cardiff, 1947).

Restagno, J. C., (ed.), *Cavalieri di San Giovanni e Territorio* (Borgighera, 1999).

Richard, J., 'Hospitals and Hospital Congregations in the Latin Kingdom during the First Period of the Frankish Conquest', in B. Z. Kedar (et al. eds.), *Outremer: Studies in the History of the Crusading Kingdom of Jerusalem Presented to Joshua Prawer* (Jerusalem, 1982), 89–100.

Richard, J., 'Les Templiers et les Hospitaliers en Bourgogne et en Champagne méridionale (XIIe–XIIIe siècle)', in *Die geistlichen Ritterordens Europoas* (Sigmaringen, 1980), 231–242.

Riley-Smith, J., *Hospitallers: The History of the Order of St John* (London, 1999).

Riley-Smith, J., *The Knights of St John in Jerusalem and Cyprus, c.1050–1310* (London, 1967).

Rodel, W. G., 'Catholic and Protestant Members of the German Grand Priory of the Order of St John: the Development of the Bailliwick of Brandenburg', in M. Barber (ed.), *The Military Orders: Fighting for the Faith and Caring for the Sick* (Aldershot, 1994), 34–41.

Sarnowsky, J., 'The Oligarchy at Work: The Chapters General of the Hospitallers in the XVth Century (1421–1522)', in M. Balard (ed.), *Autour de la Première Croisade* (Paris, 1996), 267–276.

Schermerhorn, E. W., *Malta of the Knights* (London, 1929).

Selwood, D., *Knights of the Cloister, Templers and Hospitallers in Central-Southern Occitania 1100–1300* (Woodbridge, 1999).

Short, R., 'Two Hospitaller Castles on the Island of Tilos, on the Southern Dodecanese (Megalo Horia & Agriosikia)', *Castles Study Group, Newsletter*, 15 (2002–02), 96–100.

Sinclair, K. V., *The Hospitallers' Riwle. Miracula et Regula Hospitalis Sancti Johannis Jerosolimitani (Anglo-Norman Texts, vol. 42)* (London, 1984).

Sire, H. J. A., 'The Character of the Hospitaller Properties in Spain in the Middle Ages', in M. Barber (ed.), *The Military Orders: Fighting for the Faith and Caring for the Sick* (Aldershot, 1994), 21–27.

Vann, T. M., 'The Militia of Malta', *The Journal of Medieval Military History*, 2 (2004), 137–148.

Van-Winter, J., 'Les Seigneurs de Sante-Catherine à Utrecht, les premiers Hospitaliers au nord des Alpes', in M. Balard (ed.), *Autour de la Première Croisade* (Paris, 1996), 239–246.

Williams, A., 'Crusaders as Frontiersmen: The Case of the Order of St John in the Mediterranean', in D. Power and N. Standen (eds.), *Frontiers in Questions: Eurasian Borderlands 700–1700* (Basingstoke, 1999), 209–227.

Williams, A., 'Xenodochium to Sacred Infirmary; the Changing Role of the Hospital of the Order of St John, 1522–1631', in M. Barber (ed.), *The Military Orders: Fighting for the Faith and Caring for the Sick* (Aldershot, 1994), 97–102.

Glossary

Admiral	Senior naval officer in the Order.
Afeutreüre	Felt padding or soft-armour worn beneath the hauberk.
Aketon	Quilted garment worn beneath armour.
Arbalestry	Crossbow-store.
Arcons	Extensions on a saddle that protected the rider's hips.
Arcs de bodoc	Pellet bows.
Arming cap	Padded cap worn beneath a helmet.
Arming doublet or arming jacket	Garment worn beneath armour, often with elements of mail attached.
Arming points	Laces on inner layer of armour or clothing to which plate armour is tied.
Armourer's mark	Stamp on a piece of armour indicating the manufacturer.
Aspirant	Novice wishing to become a full brother of the Order.
Auberc jaserant	Islamic hardened leather armour.
Auberge	Dormitory or barracks.
Bailli	Title of executive administrative authority.
Bailliwick	Area administrated by a bailli.
Barbute	A helmet similar to the salet but with greater protection for the face.
Barding	Horse coverings.
Barkil	A grade of rank probably referring to a turcopole.
Bascinet	Close-fitting helmet.
Bataille	Battlefield division.
Benefice	Land under the authority of a preceptor.
Bevor	Piece of armour attached to front of helmet to protect throat.
Beylik	Small, independent Turkish Islamic state.
Bezant	Gold coin based upon the coinage of the Byzantine Empire.
Bill	Form of long-hafted infantry weapon.
Biretta	Hat.

Bombarda	Type of cannon.
Brigandine	Form of scale-lined body armour.
Brother-of-the-parmentarie	Brother-in-service assisting the Drapier.
Brother-at-arms	Member of a Military Order having military duties.
Brother-at-service	Member of a Military Order having non-military duties.
Buonavoglia	Volunteer galley oarsmen.
Caignle	Strap securing the saddle.
Calcar	Raised extension or beak on the prow of a galley.
Candelabres	Strengthening frame or rim on a helmet.
Cantle	Rear part of a saddle.
Caparisons	Cloth horse coverings.
Capitular bailli	Senior bailli.
Cappa	Monastic habit; item of clothing.
Caput breve	Detailed report on a commandery drawn up by its prior.
Carrack	Large sailing ship developed in the 15th century.
Caravan	Military service or expedition, including naval service.
Casal (pl. casalia)	Village, estate.
Castellan	Officer in command of an important castle.
Cervellière	Originally the part of a helmet covering the skull; later a small, close-fitting helmet worn under a coif.
Chancellor	Senior legal official.
Chantry priest	Priest whose main duty was to recite Mass for the dead.
Chapel de fer	Brimmed helmet.
Chapelier	11th-century term for a mail coif.
Chapter	Meeting of a convent or of executive members of a religious order.
Chapter General	Governing committee of the Order.
Chausses	Mail leg protections.
Chausses avantpiés	Hose incorporating a pointed shoe.
Chevissement	A first appointment for a preceptor.
Clamida	Mantle.
Clavain	Probably the reinforced neck part of a hauberk.
Close helmet	Style of helmet with pivoted front part and pivoted visor.
Coat-of-plates	Early form of laminated or scale-lined body armour.
Coif	Head covering, of cloth or mail.
Cog	Used by the Turks to mean a carrack.
Commander of Knights	Officer who led the knights if the Marshal or his Lieutenant were not available.
Commander of the Vault	Official in charge of stores.
Commander	Officer in charge of a Hospitaller commandery.
Commandery	Smallest territorial division of the Order

(*see also* Preceptory).

Compline	The final service of the canonical hours.
Conductor	Subordinate of the preceptor.
Confrater	Layman associated with the Hospitallers.
Conrois	Tactical cavalry unit.
Constable	Senior organizational military officer.
Convent	Grouping of Hospitaller brethren, usually referring to the central convent or headquarters.
Conventual bailli	Official or bailli in the Central Convent.
Conventual Prior	The Order's most senior religious official.
Coreau de fetur	Leather cuirass.
Cote hardie	Short coat.
Cotta	Tunic.
Couched	Lowered position of a lance ready for impact in a charge.
Coutel	Dagger.
Couter	Elbow protection.
Couvertures	Protective coverings for horses.
Crie	Official who ran the stables.
Cuirasses	Leather body armour.
Cuirie	Leather body armour.
Cuisses	Quilted protection for the thighs.
Destrier	Warhorse.
Domus	Individual house, or small Hospitaller convent.
Donat	Nobleman waiting to join the Hospitallers as a full brother.
Drapier	Official in charge of clothing.
Escheated	Handed back (referring to armour).
Eschielle	Cavalry squadron.
Escrimissent	Fencing or skirmishing on foot with sword or spear.
Esgart	Legal complaint and judgement.
Espalier d'arme	Mail or padded shoulder defence.
Faussar affilé	Form of infantry weapon with a long blade.
Flanboiant	Cloth covering worn with a helmet to protect the wearer from the sun.
Fenestral	Visor of a helmet.
Fief	Estate.
Foyne	A thrust with a sword.
Frankalmoign	Freehold.
Galiote	Small galley.
Galleon	Warship.
Galoches	Large overshoes.
Gambais, gambeson	Padding under a hauberk.
Garnache	Hooded coat.

Genellières	Early form of knee protection.
Gipelle	Jupon or quilted soft armour.
Gonfalonier	Standard-bearer.
Gonfalon	Flag.
Gorget	Plated protection for the throat.
Gorgiere	Large collar on a mantle.
Grand Commander	Master's administrative second in command.
Grand Esquire	Officer in charge of the Master's own squires.
Grand Preceptor	Senior official in charge of priories in Germany, central Europe and sometimes Scandinavia.
Grange	Outlying property.
Great carrack	Large sailing ship.
Greave	Armour for the lower leg.
Guarnement	Arms and armour.
Guisarme d'acier	Long-hafted infantry axe.
Hand-and-a-half sword	Large sword that can be wielded with two hands.
Hargan	Long coat.
Hauberk	Basic mail armour for the body and usually the arms.
Hantier	Support for the butt of a lance when carried vertically.
Horarium	Sequence of daily religious services in a monastic order.
Hose	Male clothing for legs and lower body.
Hospice	Hostel, often for pilgrims.
Hospitaller	Official responsible for the sick.
Infirmarian	Official in charge of the infirmary.
Infirmary	Hospital in the modern sense.
Jupon	Tight-fitting quilted garment, originally worn beneath armour.
Justiciar	Chief Minister.
Khazaghand	Islamic hardened leather armour.
Knezat	Hungarian territorial governorate.
Langue	Basic linguistic division of the Order.
Maistre	Bowl of helmet
Manicle de fer	Integral mail mitten, forming part of mail hauberk.
Manumission	The freeing of a serf by his lord.
Mantlet	Shield.
Marshal	The most senior military official in the Order.
Marshalsy	Department run by the marshal.
Master Crossbowman	Layman in the service of the Order in charge of mercenaries.
Master Esquire	A senior brother-sergeant of the Central Convent in charge of squires, grooms and stables.
Master Sergeant	Layman in the service of the Order in charge of mercenaries.

Master	The senior figure in the Hospitaller Order.
Matins	The night or early morning service of the canonical hours.
Melee	Close combat, often after a charge.
Méliorissement	A subsequent appointment for a preceptor, higher than a chevissement.
Mensa	Food.
Mentonal	Chin-strap for a helmet.
Ministeriales	Warriors with the legal status of serfs but otherwise forming a military elite, mostly in Germany.
Misericorde	Dagger.
Missal	Book of the Mass.
Mitten	Protection for the hand without individual fingers.
Nasal	Nose protection on a helmet.
Nauclerius	Sailing master aboard a ship, but not its captain.
Nones	A mid-afternoon service of the canonical hours.
Novitiate	System of training youngsters for possible entry into a religious order.
Oblation	The placing of boys in a religious order for their education.
Oreillet	Form of hat covering the ears.
Palatinate	Territory ruled by a lord with effectively sovereign authority.
Panceriam	Lighter or more limited form of mail armour.
Parmentarie	Clothing store.
Passage particulier	A series of small assaults.
Passage général	An all-out assault.
Pauldron	Plated armour for shoulder.
Pavise	Large shield.
Pennoncelle	Small pennon.
Pilier	Senior figure in a langue or linguistic division of the Order.
Pittance	Small amount or allowance.
Plaint	Formal recital of a grievance in an esgart.
Planeau	Sandal.
Playines	Plate armour.
Points	Laces to which hose and other garments could be attached. *See also* arming points.
Poitral	Strap securing the saddle.
Poleyn	Protection for the knee.
Preceptor	Official in command of a preceptory.
Preceptory	Smallest territorial and administrative unit in the Order (*see also* Commandery).
Prior	Official in charge of a priory.
Priory	Administrative province of the Hospitaller Order.
Procurator	Senior legal and financial official of the Order.

Proofed	Tested under controlled conditions.
Quarrel	Arrow for a crossbow.
Quarantaine	Punishment of 40 days 'loss of habit'.
Quillons	Crossguard of a sword.
Quir boli	Hardened leather.
Rerebrace	Armour for the upper arm.
Riters	Knights of the German Empire.
Robes of pittance	Robes of thin cloth for use in summer.
Rondel	Probably a scarf.
Sabaton	Armour for the foot.
Salet	Open-faced helmet also covering the rear of the head.
Samit	Fine cloth.
Scutifier	Squire.
Selles d'armes	European-style war-saddles.
Seneschal	Senior military official.
Septaine	Punishment of seven days 'loss of habit'.
Serf	European of unfree status but not a slave.
Sergeant	Soldier of non-noble origin.
Soliers	Ordinary shoes.
Sorcaingles	Strap to secure a saddle.
Soubre seignal	Perhaps a surcoat.
Stabilimenta	Legislation within the Order.
Statute	A law of the Order, or a ruling by the Central Chapter of the Order.
Sub-Marshal	Assistant to the marshal.
Sub-commander	An official subordinate to the preceptor.
Surcoat	Large garment worn over armour, usually heraldic
Tabard	Small garment worn over armour, usually heraldic.
Talevaz	A very large shield. *See also* mantlet.
Tersenal	Naval arsenal of the Order at Rhodes.
Treasurer	Official in charge of the Treasury.
Tüfek	Turkish term for a hand-gun.
Turcoman	A hack or riding horse, as opposed to a warhorse.
Turcopole	Locally recruited light cavalry soldier of Near or Middle Eastern origin, serving in his traditional manner.
Turcopolier	Senior officer in command of the Order's turcopoles.
Uellière	Eye-slits on a helmet.
Usance	Custom or tradition of the Order.
Vambrace	Armour for the lower arm.
Ventail	Mail flap to protect throat and chin.
Vespers	Service of evening prayer in the canonical hours.
Voivode	Hungarian territorial governorate.

Index

Figures in bold refer to illustrations
and maps.

A

RHODES

CYPRUS   *Nicos*

Limo

M E D I T E R R A N E A N

S E A

Damietta

Alexandria

El A

ASIA MINOR,
and the
STATES OF THE CRUSADERS
in SYRIA, about 1140.
Scale 1:10000000

FATIMIT

Cairo CALIFAT

OF CAI